# MACHINE VISION SYSTEMS

## AS PER ANNA UNIVERSITY R2021 - MR3701

ANAND JAYAKUMAR ARUMUGHAM
DR. C SARAVANA MURTHI

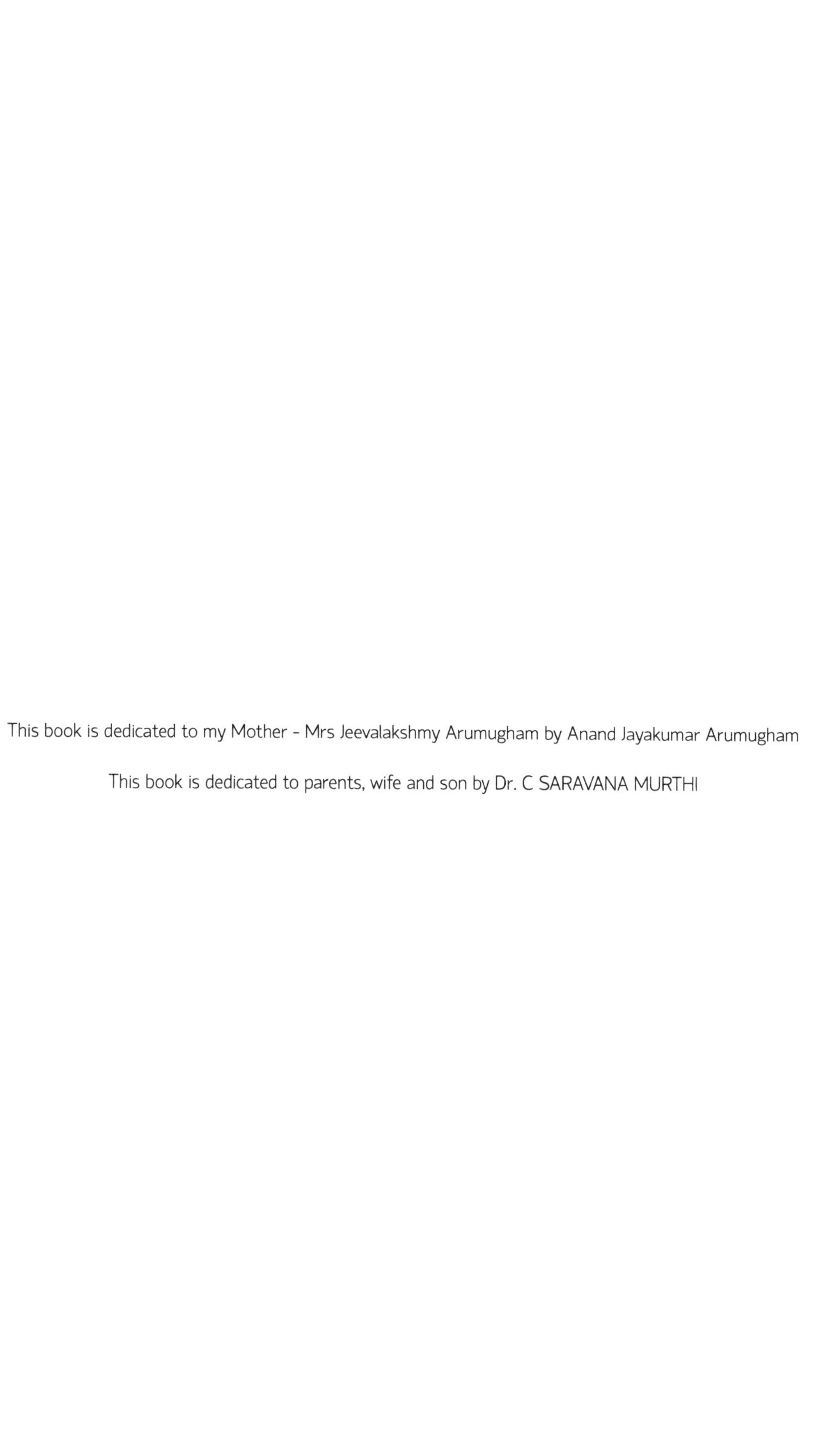

This book is dedicated to my Mother - Mrs Jeevalakshmy Arumugham by Anand Jayakumar Arumugham

This book is dedicated to parents, wife and son by Dr. C SARAVANA MURTHI

# Contents

# Contents

# Preface

In recent years, machine vision has transformed from a specialized tool into a core technology across various industries, empowering automation, enhancing precision, and redefining efficiency. This book, structured to provide a foundational understanding and practical insight into machine vision systems, guides readers through every layer of machine vision technology—laying a strong emphasis on both theoretical and application-oriented knowledge.

The first unit serves as an introduction, bridging the natural process of human vision with the intricacies of machine and computer vision. Here, readers explore the fundamental principles that drive machine vision, including system architecture and the physics of light—a cornerstone in vision applications. Moving forward, the book delves into the second unit on image acquisition, where the principles of lighting, lens selection, and camera interfaces are discussed in detail, establishing a clear understanding of image formation and camera calibration techniques crucial for high-quality visual data.

The third unit focuses on image processing, offering readers insight into the methods used to enhance and analyze images. Here, spatial and frequency domain operations are explained, and essential techniques such as thresholding, edge detection, and binary morphology are introduced, providing readers with practical tools to interpret and manipulate visual data.

Unit four tackles feature extraction, a critical aspect of machine vision where characteristics such as shape, size, texture, and color are quantified to make informed decisions. Advanced topics like 3D machine vision and classification methods allow readers to explore depth-based applications and real-world decision-making processes within machine vision systems.

The final unit presents diverse applications of machine vision, demonstrating its use in manufacturing, agriculture, medicine, and beyond. These case studies illustrate how machine vision is applied in both visible and non-visible spectrums, supporting fields from robotics to surveillance. By the end of this book, readers will have developed a comprehensive understanding of machine vision, equipped with the knowledge to implement and innovate in this rapidly evolving field.

This book is designed for students, researchers, and professionals eager to master the technology of machine vision. By emphasizing both foundational theory and practical application, it serves as a complete resource for anyone interested in the power and potential of vision-based automation.

Authors

Anand Jayakumar Arumugham - jay4upeople@gmail.com

Dr. C SARAVANA MURTHI - profcsmurthi@gmail.com

# Acknowledgements

## Acknowledgement by Anand Jayakumar Arumugham

The satisfaction and euphoria of successful completion of any task could be incomplete without mentioning the people who made it possible, whose constant guidance and encouragement crown my efforts with success.

I take this opportunity to express my sincere gratitude to the Chairman Shri.V.LAKSHMINARAYANASAMY MBA, Suguna Collage of Engineering, for providing me with a successful environment and his encouragement in the right path to develop a fine book.

I am thankful to the Secretary - Suguna Charitable Trust Dr. SRIKANTH KANNAN, for his constant encouragement and support throughout the preparation of the book.

I am thankful to my Director Dr. PRAKASAM, M.E, Ph.D., for his constant encouragement and support throughout the preparation of the book.

I are also very much grateful and would like to express my sincere thanks to my Principal Dr.R.MAGUDEESWARAN, M.E, Ph.D., who provided me with constant support and encouragement in preparing this book.

I are also very much grateful and would like to express my sincere thanks to my Head of Department Dr.R.Vasanth, M.E, Ph.D., and Assistant Head of Department Mr.N.Duraishankar, M.E, who provided me with constant support and encouragement in preparing this book.

I would like to extend my sincere thanks to all the faculty members and lab technicians for their constant support and coordination in bringing out this book.

Above all I thank my beloved mother and brother for their moral support, encouragement and their prayers during the preparation of this book.

## Acknowledgement by Dr. C SARAVANA MURTHI

The satisfaction and euphoria of successful completion of any task could be incomplete without mentioning the people who made it possible, whose constant guidance and encouragement crown my efforts with success.

I would like to take this opportunity to express my sincere gratitude to the Chairman, Shri. S. Shanmugam, B.E., M.S., of United Institute of Technology, for providing me with a supportive environment and for his guidance and encouragement in helping me develop a successful book.

I would also like to express my heartfelt gratitude to the Co-Chairman and Principal, Dr. S. Mythili, M.Tech., Ph.D., for her constant support and encouragement.

I would like to extend my sincere thanks to all the faculty members and lab technicians for their constant support.

Above all, I want to express my gratitude to my family for their prayers, encouragement, and moral support while I was writing this book.

# Prologue

As we stand on the cusp of a new era in technological advancement, the capacity of machines to "see" has sparked a revolution across fields as varied as manufacturing, medicine, and agriculture. Machine vision, once confined to experimental labs, is now an integral part of intelligent systems that transform how we interact with, interpret, and manipulate the world around us. This book embarks on a journey through the layers of machine vision technology, a domain where light, lenses, and algorithms converge to give machines an extraordinary ability: perception.

Machine vision extends beyond emulating human sight; it enables machines to detect patterns, identify flaws, and make decisions with accuracy and speed far beyond human capability. The opening chapter lays the foundation, connecting the physics of light with the intricacies of vision system architecture. Here, we explore the essence of vision itself, uncovering principles that guide light through lenses and onto sensors, creating the building blocks of machine perception.

As the book progresses, readers delve into the realm of image acquisition, an art and science of capturing scenes with the precision that machine vision demands. With topics ranging from lighting techniques to lens specifications, readers learn how to refine image quality and ensure that each frame meets the stringent standards required for further analysis. In the digital realm of image processing, algorithms work to enhance, refine, and interpret these images—enabling machines to highlight crucial details and discern meaningful patterns from raw data.

From here, the focus shifts to feature extraction, where machines analyze shapes, textures, and patterns, transforming images into actionable insights. The ability to differentiate between fine details enables everything from automated inspection in manufacturing to sophisticated medical diagnostics.

The final unit reveals the versatility of machine vision applications, from guiding robots in factories to enabling real-time surveillance, assisting in agricultural assessments, and even enhancing augmented reality experiences. Through these applications, machine vision finds a purpose in fields as diverse as industry and healthcare, offering new solutions and enhancing human potential.

This prologue is a gateway into the world of machine vision—a field poised to redefine the boundaries of automation and innovation. As we step into the chapters ahead, we invite readers to discover the transformative power of machine vision and the endless possibilities it holds for the future.

# CHAPTER ONE

# INTRODUCTION

Human vision – Machine vision and Computer vision – Benefits of machine vision – Block diagram and function of machine vision system implementation of industrial machine visionsystem – Physics of Light – Interactions of light – Refraction at a spherical surface – Thin Lens Equation

# Human Vision

Human vision is a remarkable sensory process that enables us to perceive, interpret, and interact with the world around us. It begins as light enters the eye, travels through its structures, and ultimately reaches the brain, where it is processed into images. This journey from light to perception is complex, involving multiple steps that each play a crucial role in transforming raw light into meaningful visual information.

## The Process of Human Vision

1. **Light Entry and Refraction:** Vision starts when light reflects off objects in our environment and enters the eye through a transparent layer known as the cornea. The cornea, along with the eye's lens, refracts or bends the light to focus it. This bending is necessary to concentrate light rays onto the retina, the light-sensitive layer at the back of the eye.
2. **Focusing with the Lens:** Behind the cornea, the lens further adjusts the focus, a process controlled by the ciliary muscles. This ability to change shape, known as accommodation, allows us to focus on objects at different distances, providing clear vision for both nearby and distant objects.
3. **The Retina and Photoreceptor Cells:** When light reaches the retina, it interacts with two types of specialized cells called photoreceptors: rods and cones. Rods are more sensitive to low light levels and help us see in dim lighting, while cones are responsible for color vision and detail perception. The cones are concentrated in the macula, the central part of the retina, allowing for sharp, detailed vision, especially in daylight.
4. **Conversion to Neural Signals:** Photoreceptors convert light into electrical signals through a process called phototransduction. This conversion is the beginning of interpreting light as visual data, which is then sent through the optic nerve to the brain.
5. **Visual Processing in the Brain:** The optic nerve transmits these signals to the visual cortex in the brain, located in the occipital lobe. The brain then decodes and assembles these signals, allowing us to recognize shapes, colors, movement, and depth. This sophisticated process enables us to interpret and respond to our surroundings in real time.

## Depth Perception, Color Vision, and Visual Acuity

**Depth Perception:** Our eyes work together to provide depth perception, a process called stereopsis. By combining slightly different images from each eye, the brain calculates distance, helping us perceive the world in three dimensions.

**Color Vision:** Cones in the retina allow us to see color by responding to different wavelengths of light (primarily red, green, and blue). These color signals combine, enabling us to perceive a full spectrum of colors.

**Visual Acuity:** The ability to see fine detail, known as visual acuity, is determined by the density of photoreceptors in the retina, particularly in the fovea, the central part of the macula.

## The Importance of Vision

Human vision is essential for daily functioning, helping us navigate our environment, recognize faces, read, and respond to changes. It is also deeply integrated with other cognitive processes, such as memory and attention, forming a core aspect of our experience and interaction with the world.

In summary, human vision is a complex, multi-stage process that transforms light into images we can understand. Each component of the eye and brain works in harmony to produce a seamless visual experience, enabling us to interact with the world in profound and meaningful ways. This understanding of human vision lays the groundwork for the development of machine vision, where we attempt to replicate, in machines, some of the incredible capabilities of our visual system.

# Machine vision and Computer vision

Machine vision and computer vision are closely related fields, often used interchangeably, but they have distinct applications and purposes.

## Machine Vision

Machine vision refers to the use of technology to enable machines to "see" and interpret visual information. Primarily used in industrial and manufacturing settings, machine vision systems are designed to automate inspection, quality control, and monitoring tasks. The goal is to replicate human inspection processes with higher speed, precision, and consistency.

### Key Components of Machine Vision

1. **Image Acquisition:** Machine vision systems begin with image acquisition, using cameras, lighting, and optical filters to capture images of the object or scene. Proper lighting and lenses are crucial to ensure image quality, especially in industrial environments with specific visual demands.
2. **Image Processing:** After capturing images, machine vision software processes them to extract information. Common techniques include filtering, thresholding, and edge detection to identify features like shape, size, or defects.
3. **Analysis and Decision-Making:** Machine vision systems analyze processed images to make decisions. For example, in quality inspection, a machine vision system can detect defects by comparing the object with a pre-defined model. It can then accept, reject, or flag the object based on set criteria.
4. **Output and Integration:** The final step involves relaying the system's decision or action to another part of the manufacturing process, such as marking defective items, signaling a robotic arm, or recording data for further analysis.

### Applications of Machine Vision

**Manufacturing:** Inspection for defects, assembly verification, and alignment checks.

**Pharmaceuticals:** Checking packaging, labeling, and tablet counting.

**Automotive:** Part identification, surface inspection, and robotic guidance.

**Electronics:** Circuit board inspection, soldering verification, and component alignment.

Machine vision is optimized for specific tasks in controlled environments, ensuring precision and reliability. Its focus is on practical applications and high-volume inspection, typically operating in real-time.

## Computer Vision

Computer vision is a broader field within artificial intelligence (AI) that focuses on enabling computers to interpret and understand visual information. Unlike machine vision, which is often limited to specific tasks, computer vision aims to replicate human vision capabilities and goes beyond to develop general algorithms that enable a wide range of image and video analysis.

### Key Techniques in Computer Vision

1. **Object Detection and Recognition:** Identifying and classifying objects within images or video. This is commonly used in autonomous vehicles, where systems must detect pedestrians, signs, and obstacles.
2. **Image Classification:** Assigning a label or category to an entire image, often used in image search and content moderation. For example, classifying an image as a "dog" or "cat" based on its contents.
3. **Segmentation:** Dividing an image into meaningful parts or regions to analyze structures or objects within it. Image segmentation is used in medical imaging to detect tumors or in autonomous vehicles for road segmentation.
4. **Facial Recognition:** Detecting and recognizing human faces, commonly used in security systems and biometric applications.
5. **3D Vision:** Reconstructing 3D information from 2D images, allowing for depth perception and spatial understanding. This is important in augmented reality and virtual reality applications.

## Applications of Computer Vision

**Healthcare:** Assisting in medical diagnosis, detecting abnormalities in imaging, and surgery assistance.

**Autonomous Vehicles:** Enabling navigation, obstacle detection, and lane recognition.

**Retail:** Powering checkout-free stores, inventory management, and customer analysis.

**Agriculture:** Monitoring crop health, soil analysis, and livestock management.

**Security and Surveillance:** Identifying objects, people, and abnormal activities in real-time footage.

## Differences Between Machine Vision and Computer Vision

While both fields share overlapping techniques, their primary differences lie in their applications and flexibility:

**Scope and Application:** Machine vision is specialized for specific industrial tasks, while computer vision has a wider range of applications and is more research-oriented, aimed at general-purpose image understanding.

**Environment:** Machine vision typically works in controlled environments where lighting, positioning, and other variables are standardized. Computer vision, however, is designed to handle variability, often working with images from real-world environments.

**Complexity and Flexibility:** Machine vision often uses simpler algorithms for high-speed inspection tasks, whereas computer vision incorporates advanced AI techniques like deep learning to handle more complex, unstructured data.

In summary, machine vision focuses on industrial applications and process automation, often in a controlled environment, while computer vision has a broader focus on image interpretation, replicating human vision for a variety of complex and dynamic tasks. Both fields are powerful in their respective applications, advancing automation and intelligent analysis in unique ways.

# Benefits of machine vision

Machine vision offers numerous benefits, particularly in industries that require high precision, speed, and consistency. Here are some of the key advantages:

### 1. Enhanced Quality Control

- **Defect Detection:** Machine vision systems can inspect products at a microscopic level, detecting defects or inconsistencies that may be missed by human inspectors.
- **Consistent Inspection Standards:** Unlike human inspection, machine vision systems apply the same criteria across all items, ensuring consistent quality and reducing the risk of variability.

### 2. Increased Speed and Efficiency

- **Faster Processing:** Machine vision systems can process images and make decisions in milliseconds, enabling high-speed inspection on production lines and reducing bottlenecks.
- **24/7 Operation:** Machine vision systems can operate continuously, increasing throughput and productivity without fatigue, ideal for high-volume production environments.

### 3. Cost Savings

- **Reduced Labor Costs:** By automating inspection and sorting processes, machine vision minimizes the need for manual labor, which lowers labor costs and reduces the potential for human error.
- **Waste Reduction:** Machine vision helps identify defects early in the production process, reducing waste by preventing flawed products from advancing down the line.

### 4. Improved Precision and Accuracy

- **High Accuracy:** Machine vision systems can measure dimensions, alignments, and other features with high precision, ensuring products meet exact specifications.
- **Repeatability:** Unlike human inspectors, machine vision systems are immune to fatigue or subjective interpretation, providing a repeatable and reliable inspection process.

### 5. Enhanced Safety and Compliance

- **Safer Work Environment:** Machine vision can handle tasks in hazardous environments, such as exposure to extreme temperatures, chemicals, or heavy machinery, reducing risks for human workers.
- **Regulatory Compliance:** In industries like pharmaceuticals and food production, machine vision systems help ensure products meet regulatory standards, verifying labeling accuracy, packaging integrity, and more.

### 6. Data Collection and Analysis

- **Real-Time Monitoring:** Machine vision systems provide real-time feedback, allowing manufacturers to monitor processes and make adjustments on the fly.

- **Data-Driven Insights:** Machine vision systems collect vast amounts of data, which can be analyzed for insights into quality trends, equipment performance, and process improvements.

## 7. Flexibility and Scalability

- **Easily Programmable:** Machine vision systems can be reprogrammed or reconfigured for different tasks or products, making them adaptable to changing production needs.
- **Scalable Across Operations:** Once a machine vision solution is implemented and optimized, it can be scaled across multiple production lines or facilities, standardizing processes and improving overall productivity.

## 8. Enhanced Decision-Making for Automation

- **Integration with Robotics:** Machine vision systems provide guidance for robotic arms in assembly, packaging, and material handling. This synergy enhances automation capabilities and allows for more complex tasks, like vision-guided robotics.
- **Process Control:** With continuous monitoring, machine vision systems can trigger automated responses, such as stopping a line or adjusting a machine, to maintain optimal production quality.

In summary, machine vision boosts productivity, reduces costs, enhances safety, and ensures consistent quality, providing a powerful tool for industries looking to streamline operations and stay competitive.

# Block Diagram of Machine Vision System

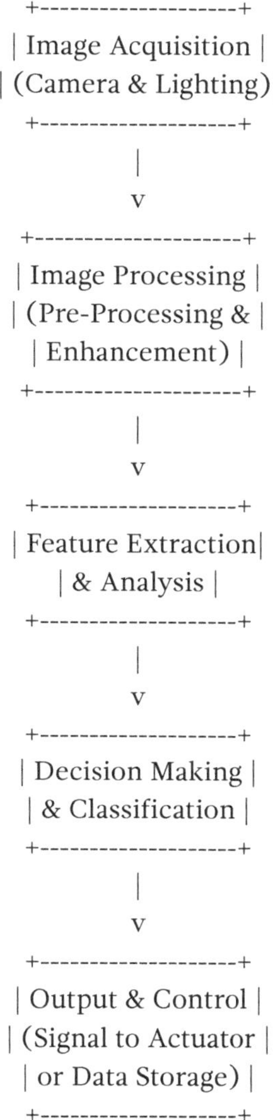

```
+-------------------+
| Image Acquisition |
| (Camera & Lighting)|
+-------------------+
          |
          v
+--------------------+
| Image Processing |
| (Pre-Processing & |
|   Enhancement) |
+--------------------+
          |
          v
+-------------------+
| Feature Extraction|
|   & Analysis |
+-------------------+
          |
          v
+-------------------+
| Decision Making |
|  & Classification |
+-------------------+
          |
          v
+-------------------+
| Output & Control |
| (Signal to Actuator |
|  or Data Storage) |
+-------------------+
```

**Components Breakdown**

**Image Acquisition:**

- This block includes the camera(s) and lighting system, capturing images of the object or scene.
- Lighting techniques are essential for clear and consistent imaging, while lenses and filters refine image clarity and focus.

**Image Processing:**

- This block enhances the image for further analysis.
- Techniques such as filtering, noise reduction, and contrast adjustments prepare the image for accurate feature extraction.

## Feature Extraction & Analysis:

- Important characteristics of the image, such as edges, shapes, textures, and regions, are extracted.
- This data represents identifiable features necessary for evaluating the object's qualities or defects.

## Decision Making & Classification:

- Here, the system decides based on pre-set criteria, determining whether the object meets specifications or should be classified as defective.
- Classification models or threshold values guide the decision-making process.

## Output & Control:

- The system sends signals to other equipment (e.g., robotic arms, sorting mechanisms) or records data for quality tracking.
- This step finalizes the inspection process and communicates results to other devices in the production line.

Each block is designed to perform a specific function, allowing the machine vision system to work seamlessly for applications such as quality inspection, defect detection, and robotic guidance.

# Function of machine vision system

The primary function of a machine vision system is to enable automated visual inspection, measurement, and decision-making by processing and analyzing images of objects. This system replicates certain aspects of human vision to perform tasks more consistently, quickly, and accurately. Below is a breakdown of the main functions of a machine vision system:

### 1. Image Acquisition

- The first function of a machine vision system is capturing images of the object or scene, using cameras, lenses, and appropriate lighting.
- Cameras take snapshots or continuous video, while lighting enhances visibility and highlights relevant features.
- Proper lighting, lenses, and positioning ensure that the images captured are of high quality and suitable for further analysis.

### 2. Image Pre-Processing

- Once the image is acquired, it undergoes pre-processing to enhance quality and remove unwanted noise.
- This function may involve filtering (to reduce noise), contrast adjustment, and grayscale conversion.
- The goal is to make specific features of the image clearer, setting it up for accurate analysis in the subsequent steps.

### 3. Feature Extraction

- After pre-processing, the system identifies and extracts important features such as edges, shapes, textures, or colors that are relevant to the inspection task.
- Commonly used techniques include edge detection, blob analysis, contour tracing, and thresholding to separate regions or objects of interest.
- This step converts visual information into quantifiable data, such as dimensions, shapes, or patterns, that can be used in decision-making.

### 4. Pattern Recognition and Classification

- In this stage, the system compares extracted features with predefined criteria or reference models to recognize patterns, shapes, or objects.
- Pattern matching techniques are used to verify that parts meet expected specifications, while classification methods categorize objects (e.g., defective vs. acceptable items).
- This function is essential in applications like quality control, where items are sorted based on similarity or adherence to specifications.

### 5. Decision Making

- Based on the analysis, the system makes a decision, such as accepting or rejecting a part, measuring dimensions, or detecting defects.

- Rules, algorithms, or AI models guide this decision-making process, allowing the system to distinguish between acceptable and unacceptable items based on set criteria.
  - For example, in manufacturing, a machine vision system might detect missing components, size mismatches, or surface defects and then categorize each item accordingly.

## 6. Output and Control

- After making a decision, the system generates an output that can trigger actions like notifying a defect, actuating a robotic arm, or updating a quality log.
- Outputs can be in the form of signals sent to other equipment, visual alerts, or data stored for analysis and reporting.
- This function allows machine vision systems to interact with other machines, enabling automation and integration into larger production systems.

## 7. Data Storage and Feedback Loop

- Many machine vision systems store data for analysis, which can provide valuable insights into production trends, defect rates, and process improvements.
- In a feedback loop, the data can be used to adjust parameters in real-time, improving the inspection or measurement process continuously.

## Summary

In summary, the functions of a machine vision system include:

- **Image Acquisition:** Capturing high-quality images.
- **Pre-Processing:** Enhancing images for better feature visibility.
- **Feature Extraction:** Identifying essential features in the image.
- **Pattern Recognition & Classification:** Recognizing and categorizing objects based on set criteria.
- **Decision Making:** Determining the status (e.g., pass/fail) based on analyzed data.
- **Output & Control:** Triggering actions or alerts based on decisions made.
- **Data Storage & Feedback:** Storing data for analysis and continuous improvement.

By performing these functions, machine vision systems automate inspection, quality control, measurement, and more, increasing productivity, consistency, and accuracy in various applications across industries.

# Implementation of industrial machine vision system

Implementing an industrial machine vision system involves a systematic process of selecting, designing, and configuring components to ensure accurate and reliable performance in specific industrial applications. Here's a step-by-step outline of how an industrial machine vision system is typically implemented:

### 1. Define System Requirements

- **Understand the Application:** Clearly define the purpose of the machine vision system. Common applications include quality inspection, part identification, alignment verification, and measurement.
- **Identify Key Performance Metrics:** Set requirements for speed, accuracy, resolution, and the level of detail needed. For example, a high-speed production line will need faster processing capabilities than a slower line with high-detail inspection needs.
- **Environmental Considerations:** Consider factors like lighting conditions, temperature, vibration, dust, or humidity, as these can affect image quality and system durability.

### 2. Choose the Image Acquisition Components

- **Camera Selection:** Choose between CCD (Charge-Coupled Device) or CMOS (Complementary Metal-Oxide Semiconductor) cameras based on factors like resolution, speed, and lighting conditions.
  - **Resolution:** Higher resolutions allow for more detail but may require more processing power.
  - **Frame Rate:** High frame rates are necessary for capturing fast-moving objects in real-time.
  - **Lighting Setup:** Select appropriate lighting sources (LED, halogen, fluorescent) and techniques (backlighting, front lighting, structured lighting) to improve image contrast and highlight specific features.
- **Lens Selection:** Select lenses based on focal length, field of view, and depth of field. For instance, a telecentric lens minimizes distortion, which is crucial for measurement applications.
- **Optical Filters:** Filters can improve image quality by blocking unwanted wavelengths or enhancing contrast, depending on the application.

### 3. Set Up Image Processing Software

- **Software Selection:** Use dedicated machine vision software or a custom solution that provides image analysis tools like edge detection, filtering, pattern matching, and feature extraction.
- **Algorithm Development:** Develop and test algorithms tailored to the specific tasks of the application. Algorithms may include thresholding, edge detection, blob analysis, and pattern recognition.
- **Calibration and Correction:** Calibrate the system to account for optical distortions or alignment errors. Camera calibration is essential for accurate measurements, particularly in applications requiring high precision.

### 4. Integrate Feature Extraction and Analysis

- **Feature Identification:** Configure the software to identify key features relevant to the task, such as dimensions, color, shape, or surface texture.
- **Parameter Setting:** Set acceptable tolerances for each feature, allowing the system to determine pass/fail criteria.

- **Train Classification Models:** For complex applications, machine learning or AI-based classification models can be trained to recognize objects, detect defects, or categorize products.

## 5. Establish Decision-Making Logic

- **Define Rules and Criteria:** Program decision-making logic based on inspection results. For example, establish criteria for accepting, rejecting, or categorizing items based on measurement or feature matching results.
- **Integrate with Quality Control:** Ensure that decisions made by the system align with the organization's quality standards and production goals.

## 6. Configure Output and Control Systems

- **Communication Protocols:** Set up communication protocols (e.g., Ethernet, USB, RS-232) to transmit data from the machine vision system to other devices or systems.
- **Output Signals:** Configure the system to send output signals to controllers, such as triggering a robotic arm, rejecting defective parts, or marking items for further inspection.
- **Data Logging and Analysis:** Store inspection data for tracking quality trends, improving processes, or complying with regulatory requirements.

## 7. Testing and Validation

- **System Testing:** Run tests to ensure that the system meets speed, accuracy, and reliability requirements. Use sample products or test cases to confirm system performance under production conditions.
- **Environmental Testing:** Test the system in the actual production environment, accounting for variables like lighting, vibration, and changes in temperature.
- **Fine-Tuning:** Make adjustments based on test results, such as tweaking lighting angles, adjusting camera positioning, or refining algorithm parameters.

## 8. Implementation and Integration

- **Integrate with Production Line:** Implement the machine vision system in its designated location on the production line. Ensure that it is correctly positioned and synchronized with other automated systems.
- **Operator Training:** Train personnel on system operation, including troubleshooting basic issues and interpreting results.
- **Set Up Maintenance Protocols:** Establish regular maintenance schedules to clean cameras and lenses, recalibrate as needed, and update software or algorithms for optimal performance.

## 9. Monitor and Optimize

- **Real-Time Monitoring:** Set up real-time monitoring to track system performance, analyze data, and detect any trends that could signal issues or opportunities for improvement.
- **Continuous Improvement:** Based on operational data, optimize system parameters and algorithms over time to maintain accuracy and efficiency as production demands or conditions change.
- **Feedback Loop:** Utilize data insights to inform adjustments, either in the machine vision system or upstream in the production process, to improve overall quality and efficiency.

## Summary

Implementing an industrial machine vision system is a systematic process involving:

- Defining Requirements based on application and environment,
- Choosing and Configuring Hardware for image acquisition,
- Developing and Integrating Software for image processing, feature extraction, and decision-making,
- Testing and Validating to ensure the system meets production demands,
- Implementing and Integrating into the production line, and
- Monitoring and Optimizing for continuous improvement.

By following these steps, a machine vision system can be tailored to specific industrial applications, delivering improved accuracy, speed, and quality in automated processes.

# Physics of Light

The physics of light is fundamental to understanding how vision systems—both human and machine—interpret visual information. Light is an electromagnetic wave that behaves both as a particle (photon) and as a wave. This wave-particle duality of light is crucial for various optical phenomena, including reflection, refraction, dispersion, and diffraction. Here's a breakdown of key concepts related to the physics of light:

## 1. Nature of Light

- Light is part of the electromagnetic spectrum, which includes other waves such as radio waves, microwaves, infrared, ultraviolet, X-rays, and gamma rays.
- The visible spectrum is the portion of the electromagnetic spectrum detectable by the human eye, ranging from approximately 400 nm (violet) to 700 nm (red) in wavelength.
- Photon Theory: Light can be described as photons, which are particles of light that carry energy. The energy of a photon is directly proportional to the light's frequency.

## 2. Reflection of Light

- Reflection occurs when light rays strike a surface and bounce back. The law of reflection states that the angle of incidence (the angle between the incoming light ray and the normal to the surface) is equal to the angle of reflection (the angle between the reflected ray and the normal).
- Reflection can be specular (smooth surfaces, like mirrors) or diffuse (rough surfaces, like paper). Specular reflection retains image quality, while diffuse reflection scatters light in multiple directions.

## 3. Refraction of Light

- Refraction is the bending of light as it passes from one medium to another with a different density (e.g., air to water).
- This bending occurs because light changes speed as it moves from one medium to another. The relationship between the angles of incidence and refraction is governed by Snell's Law: $n_1 \sin(\theta_1) = n_2 \sin(\theta_2)$ where $n_1$ and $n_2$ are the refractive indices of the two media, and $\theta_1$ and $\theta_2$ are the angles of incidence and refraction, respectively.
- The refractive index ($nnn$) of a medium measures how much light slows down in that medium. For example, water has a refractive index of 1.33, meaning light slows down to about 75% of its speed in a vacuum when it enters water.

## 4. Dispersion of Light

- Dispersion is the separation of light into its component colors (wavelengths), typically seen when light passes through a prism. Each wavelength bends at a slightly different angle, causing the colors to spread out and form a spectrum.
- This occurs because different wavelengths of light refract at slightly different angles when passing through a medium.

## 5. Diffraction of Light

- Diffraction is the bending of light around the edges of an object or through a narrow opening. It is more pronounced when the size of the object or opening is comparable to the wavelength of light.
- Diffraction patterns (e.g., interference fringes) occur when light waves spread out and interfere with each other, resulting in areas of constructive (bright) and destructive (dark) interference.

## 6. Interference of Light

- Interference occurs when two or more light waves overlap, producing regions of constructive interference (where the waves amplify each other) and destructive interference (where they cancel each other out).
- Examples of interference include soap bubbles and oil films, where varying colors are visible due to thin-film interference.

## 7. Polarization of Light

- Polarization is the orientation of light waves. In unpolarized light, the waves oscillate in all directions perpendicular to the direction of travel. Polarized light oscillates in only one direction.
- Polarization can be achieved through filters, reflection, or scattering and is commonly used in sunglasses and camera lenses to reduce glare.

## 8. Light Intensity and Brightness

- Intensity refers to the amount of energy a light wave carries per unit area per unit time. It's proportional to the square of the wave's amplitude.
- Brightness is the perceived intensity of light by the human eye, which is subjective and depends on the light source and ambient lighting conditions.

## 9. The Thin Lens Equation and Image Formation

- Lenses focus or disperse light rays using refraction. A convex lens converges light rays to a focal point, while a concave lens diverges them.
- The Thin Lens Equation relates the object distance (do), image distance (di), and focal length (f) of the lens: $1/f = 1/do + 1/di$
- This equation is critical in optical systems, such as cameras and machine vision systems, to determine image size and position.

## 10. Applications in Machine Vision

- Reflection and Refraction are crucial in controlling how light interacts with objects in machine vision, determining how features like edges, textures, or defects appear.
- Dispersion and Diffraction affect image quality and may need to be minimized or controlled for clearer image capture.
- Polarization helps reduce glare or reflections, improving visibility of surfaces in machine vision.
- Thin Lens Equation guides the selection of lenses to ensure the correct focal length and field of view for the application.

**Summary**

The physics of light encompasses the study of light's behavior as it interacts with various materials and boundaries. In machine vision, understanding these properties helps optimize imaging setups, such as choosing the right lenses, lighting, and filters. By mastering light's behavior, machine vision systems can achieve clearer, more accurate images for analysis, making them more effective in applications like quality inspection, measurement, and automation.

# Interactions of light

The interactions of light with different materials and surfaces are fundamental to understanding and controlling imaging processes in fields like optics and machine vision. When light encounters a medium, it can undergo several types of interactions, each affecting how the light propagates, its intensity, color, or direction. Here's a detailed look at the main types of light interactions:

## 1. Reflection

- **Definition:** Reflection occurs when light waves bounce off the surface of a material instead of passing through it. The angle at which light hits the surface (angle of incidence) is equal to the angle at which it reflects (angle of reflection), according to the law of reflection.
  - **Types of Reflection:**
  - **Specular Reflection:** Occurs on smooth, polished surfaces (like mirrors or glass). The reflection is mirror-like, retaining image clarity and detail.
  - **Diffuse Reflection:** Occurs on rough surfaces, where light is scattered in many directions, creating a matte appearance with no specific image.
- **Applications in Machine Vision:** Controlled lighting and reflective surfaces can enhance image quality. For example, diffuse lighting minimizes shadows and glare on rough surfaces, while specular lighting highlights surface details like scratches or texture.

## 2. Refraction

- **Definition:** Refraction is the bending of light as it passes from one transparent medium to another with a different density (e.g., air to water or glass). This bending occurs because light changes speed as it enters a new medium.
  - **Key Principle:** Snell's Law defines the relationship between the angles of incidence and refraction: $n1\sin(\theta1)=n2\sin(\theta2)$ where $n1$ and $n2$ are the refractive indices of the two media, and $\theta1$ and $\theta2$ are the angles of incidence and refraction.
- **Applications in Machine Vision:** Refraction is essential in focusing light through lenses. By adjusting the curvature of lenses, machine vision systems can achieve desired focal lengths, enabling sharp, clear imaging of objects at various distances.

## 3. Absorption

- **Definition:** Absorption occurs when light is taken up by a material, causing the light's energy to transfer to the material, often raising its temperature. As light energy is absorbed, the material may emit it in other forms, like heat or fluorescence.
- **Selective Absorption:** Different materials absorb different wavelengths of light. For example, a red object absorbs all visible wavelengths except red, which it reflects.
- **Applications in Machine Vision:** Understanding absorption properties helps in selecting proper lighting for contrast enhancement. For example, infrared light can penetrate certain materials better, making it useful for inspecting objects with internal components or materials that are opaque to visible light.

## 4. Transmission

- **Definition:** Transmission is the passage of light through a material. Transparent materials (like clear glass) allow most light to pass through, while translucent materials scatter some light, and opaque materials block it entirely.
- **Influence of Material Properties:** Transmission depends on the material's thickness, surface smoothness, and refractive index. Tinted materials may transmit certain wavelengths while blocking others.
- **Applications in Machine Vision:** Transmitted lighting (backlighting) is used in machine vision to create silhouettes for measuring object shapes or checking edges. Transparent or translucent materials are also chosen for optical filters, which selectively transmit specific wavelengths to enhance certain features in an image.

## 5. Scattering

- **Definition:** Scattering occurs when light encounters small particles or irregularities within a material, causing the light to disperse in multiple directions. This effect is more pronounced when the size of the particles is comparable to the wavelength of light.
  - **Types of Scattering:**
- **Rayleigh Scattering:** Light scattering from particles much smaller than its wavelength, responsible for the blue color of the sky.
- **Mie Scattering:** Light scattering from particles about the same size as its wavelength, often seen in fog or milk.
  - **Applications in Machine Vision:** Scattering affects image clarity and contrast. For instance, diffused lighting uses scattering to eliminate shadows and glare, creating a more evenly lit scene for inspection.

## 6. Diffraction

- **Definition:** Diffraction is the bending of light around obstacles or through small openings, causing it to spread out and interfere. This interaction results in a pattern of constructive (bright) and destructive (dark) interference.
  - **Conditions:** Diffraction is more noticeable when the size of the obstacle or aperture is close to the wavelength of light.
  - **Applications in Machine Vision:** In certain imaging setups, diffraction effects can cause blurring or unwanted patterns. Special care must be taken with aperture size and lens quality to minimize diffraction for high-resolution imaging.

## 7. Polarization

- **Definition:** Polarization is the orientation of the oscillations of light waves in a single plane. Natural light is unpolarized, with waves oscillating in all directions perpendicular to the direction of travel. Polarization filters or specific interactions can restrict light to oscillate in only one direction.
  - **Types of Polarization:**
  - **Linear Polarization:** Restricts light to oscillate in a single plane.
  - **Circular and Elliptical Polarization:** Light oscillates in a helical pattern, either clockwise or counterclockwise.
  - **Applications in Machine Vision:** Polarized light can reduce glare from reflective surfaces, enhance contrast, and reveal surface details like scratches or textures. Polarizing filters are frequently used in machine vision systems to improve image clarity, especially when inspecting reflective or transparent

objects.

## 8. Fluorescence and Phosphorescence

- **Fluorescence:** A material absorbs light (usually UV) and almost immediately re-emits it at a longer wavelength, visible as fluorescence. This emission stops when the light source is removed.
- **Phosphorescence:** Similar to fluorescence, but the re-emission continues for some time after the light source is removed due to delayed energy release.
- **Applications in Machine Vision:** Fluorescence is used in machine vision for marking and detecting specific substances, especially in fields like pharmaceutical inspection and biological analysis, where substances emit distinct fluorescent signatures.

## Summary of Interactions of Light in Machine Vision

Each interaction—reflection, refraction, absorption, transmission, scattering, diffraction, polarization, and fluorescence—plays a role in how machine vision systems capture, process, and interpret images. By controlling these interactions through the selection of appropriate lighting, filters, lenses, and other optical elements, machine vision systems achieve the necessary image quality and contrast to reliably perform tasks like inspection, measurement, and quality control in industrial applications.

# Refraction at a spherical surface

Refraction at a spherical surface occurs when light passes from one medium into another through a curved (spherical) surface, causing the light to bend and change direction. This bending of light due to refraction is governed by the change in light's speed between the two media and the curvature of the spherical surface. This principle is critical in optics, especially for lenses, where spherical surfaces are used to focus or diverge light.

**Key Concepts in Refraction at a Spherical Surface**

**1. Understanding Spherical Surfaces**

- A spherical surface is a part of a sphere, and it can be either convex (curved outward) or concave (curved inward).
  - These surfaces are commonly found in lenses, such as in cameras and vision systems, and they are essential for focusing or diverging light.

**2. Refraction and the Laws of Refraction**

- When light passes from one medium (like air) into another (like glass), it bends according to Snell's Law: $n_1 \sin(\theta_1) = n_2 \sin(\theta_2)$ where $n_1$ and $n_2$ are the refractive indices of the two media, and $\theta_1$ and $\theta_2$ are the angles of incidence and refraction, respectively.
  - The degree of bending depends on the change in refractive index and the angle of incidence.

**3. Derivation of the Refraction Formula for a Spherical Surface**

- When light passes through a spherical surface, the curvature of the surface affects the way light rays converge or diverge.
- For a light ray incident on a spherical surface separating two media (with refractive indices $n_1$ and $n_2$), and with the object at a distance $u$ from the surface and the image at a distance $v$, the refraction formula at a spherical surface is: $n_2/v - n_1/u = (n_2 - n_1)/R$ where:
  - R is the radius of curvature of the spherical surface,
  - u is the distance from the object to the spherical surface,
  - v is the distance from the image to the spherical surface.

**4. Convex and Concave Spherical Surfaces**

- **Convex Surface:** Light refracts through a surface that curves outward. Convex surfaces generally cause parallel light rays to converge to a focal point, depending on the curvature and the refractive indices of the media.
  - **Concave Surface:** Light refracts through a surface that curves inward, causing parallel light rays to diverge. This divergence creates a virtual focus, where rays appear to originate from a focal point on the opposite side.

**5. Sign Conventions**

- **Object Distance (u):** Measured from the pole (the central point on the surface) to the object. It is positive if the object is on the same side as the incoming light.
- **Image Distance (v):** Measured from the pole to the image. It is positive if the image forms on the side of the outgoing light.
- **Radius of Curvature (R):** Positive for convex surfaces (center of curvature is on the outgoing side of light) and negative for concave surfaces.

### Applications in Lenses and Optics

The refraction at spherical surfaces is foundational to the design and function of lenses:

- **Convex Lenses (Converging):** Use two convex spherical surfaces to bend light rays inward, focusing them to a point. This property is essential in cameras, microscopes, and corrective lenses.
- **Concave Lenses (Diverging):** Use concave spherical surfaces to spread light rays outward, creating a virtual focus. Concave lenses are often used in vision correction for conditions like myopia (nearsightedness).

### Practical Example: Using Refraction at a Spherical Surface in Machine Vision

In a machine vision system, lenses with spherical surfaces help control focus and magnification. The degree of refraction (and hence, focusing ability) is determined by the curvature of these surfaces and the refractive index of the lens material. By selecting lenses with specific radii of curvature and refractive indices, machine vision systems can achieve the required image resolution, focus, and field of view, enabling accurate inspection, measurement, and analysis of objects.

### Summary

Refraction at a spherical surface involves light bending as it moves between two media through a curved surface, governed by the refractive indices and the curvature radius of the surface. This principle is crucial in lens design, focusing, and imaging applications in optics and machine vision, enabling systems to control how light rays converge or diverge to form clear, accurate images.

# Thin Lens Equation

The Thin Lens Equation is a formula used to relate the focal length of a lens to the distances of an object from the lens and the distance of the image formed by the lens. It's a fundamental concept in optics, especially relevant for understanding how lenses work to focus light and create images in systems like cameras, microscopes, and machine vision setups.

**Thin Lens Equation**

The Thin Lens Equation is expressed as:

$$1/f = 1/d_o + 1/d_i$$

where:

- f = focal length of the lens (the distance from the lens where parallel rays converge),
  - do = object distance (the distance from the object to the lens),
  - di = image distance (the distance from the lens to the image).

This equation applies to both convex (converging) and concave (diverging) lenses, though the signs of distances and focal lengths may differ based on the type of lens and the chosen sign convention.

**Key Concepts in the Thin Lens Equation**

**Focal Length (f)**

- The focal length of a lens is a measure of its ability to converge or diverge light rays. For a convex lens, the focal length is positive, and for a concave lens, it is negative.
- The shorter the focal length, the more the lens bends light rays, allowing it to form images closer to the lens.

**Object Distance (d_o)**

- The object distance is the distance between the object being viewed and the lens. In most setups, this is measured from the object's center to the lens's center.

**Image Distance (d_i)**

- The image distance is the distance from the lens to where the image of the object is formed. For real images, this distance is positive, and for virtual images, it is negative (in typical sign conventions).

**Sign Conventions**

The Thin Lens Equation uses specific sign conventions:

- **Convex Lenses:** Focal length (f) is positive; these lenses produce real, inverted images when the object is placed beyond the focal point.

- **Concave Lenses:** Focal length (f) is negative; these lenses typically produce virtual, upright, and reduced images.
- **Image Distance (di):** Positive for real images (on the opposite side of the object) and negative for virtual images (same side as the object).
    - **Object Distance (do):** Positive if the object is on the same side as the incoming light.

## Using the Thin Lens Equation

**Finding the Image Distance:** Given the object distance and focal length, you can rearrange the Thin Lens Equation to solve for the image distance:

$$di=1/(1/f-1/do)$$

**Finding the Object Distance:** Similarly, if you know the focal length and image distance, you can solve for the object distance:

$$do=1/(1/f-1/di)$$

**Determining Magnification:** The magnification mmm of the image is given by:

$$m=-di/do$$

where a positive magnification indicates an upright image, while a negative magnification indicates an inverted image.

## Example Applications of the Thin Lens Equation

- **Cameras:** Cameras use convex lenses to focus light from an object at a distance dod_odo onto an image sensor located at did_idi. By adjusting the lens, cameras can control did_idi and produce clear images of objects at various distances.
- **Machine Vision Systems:** Machine vision lenses are selected based on the focal length needed to achieve the required image size and clarity. Using the Thin Lens Equation helps in calculating the precise lens specifications to accurately capture objects at specific distances.
- **Microscopes and Telescopes:** Microscopes use lenses with short focal lengths to enlarge close objects, while telescopes use longer focal lengths to focus distant objects.

## Practical Example

Suppose a convex lens has a focal length of 10 cm and an object is placed 15 cm from the lens. We can find the image distance (di) as follows:

$$1/f=1/do+1/di$$

$$1/10=1/15+1/di$$

Rearranging to solve for di,

$$1/di = 1/10-1/15$$

$$= (3-2)/30$$

$$= 1/30$$

$$d_i = 30 \text{ cm}$$

So, the image forms 30 cm on the opposite side of the lens, making it a real and inverted image.

## Summary

The Thin Lens Equation is a crucial formula in optics, helping to relate focal length, object distance, and image distance. By understanding and applying this equation, we can determine how lenses will form images, guiding the design of optical systems in applications from photography to scientific imaging and machine vision.

# 2 Mark Questions

1. Define human vision.
2. What is machine vision?
3. How does computer vision differ from machine vision?
4. List two benefits of machine vision in industrial applications.
5. Draw a simple block diagram of a machine vision system.
6. Describe the main function of a machine vision system.
7. What are the primary components of a machine vision system?
8. What is the role of lighting in machine vision?
9. Explain the term "Physics of Light" in the context of machine vision.
10. Name two interactions of light with matter.
11. What is meant by "reflection" of light?
12. Define "refraction" of light.
13. What happens to light when it passes through a convex lens?
14. State the Thin Lens Equation.
15. Explain "refraction at a spherical surface" in simple terms.
16. What is the purpose of the Thin Lens Equation in optics?
17. How does machine vision enhance quality control in industries?
18. What is the importance of feature extraction in machine vision?
19. Describe one application of machine vision in the automotive industry.
20. How does the block diagram of a machine vision system help in its implementation?

# 15 Mark Questions

1. Explain human vision in detail and discuss how it differs from machine vision and computer vision. What are the challenges and advantages of replicating human vision in machines?
2. Discuss the benefits of machine vision in industrial applications. How does machine vision contribute to productivity, accuracy, and quality control in various industries? Provide examples to support your answer.
3. Draw and describe the block diagram of a machine vision system. Explain the function of each component in the system and how they work together to perform visual tasks in an industrial setting.
4. Describe the process of implementing a machine vision system in an industrial environment. What factors must be considered, and how are different system components selected to meet specific application requirements?
5. Explain the physics of light in the context of machine vision. Discuss how properties of light such as wavelength, frequency, and energy influence imaging and detection in machine vision systems.
6. Describe the various interactions of light (reflection, refraction, transmission, absorption, scattering, and diffraction) and their significance in machine vision. How can these interactions be controlled to improve image quality and accuracy?
7. Explain the concept of refraction at a spherical surface. Derive the equation for refraction at a spherical surface and discuss its applications in lens design and image focusing.
8. Discuss the Thin Lens Equation and its importance in optics. Derive the equation and explain how it is applied to determine the focal length, object distance, and image distance in machine vision and optical systems.
9. Compare and contrast human vision, machine vision, and computer vision in terms of their components, processes, and applications. What are the limitations of each, and how do they complement each other in practical use?
10. Discuss the importance of lighting and optics in machine vision systems. How does proper selection of lighting techniques, lenses, and optical filters affect the accuracy and effectiveness of a machine vision system?

# IMAGE ACQUISITION

Scene constraints – Lighting parameters – Lighting sources, Selection – Lighting Techniques – Types and Selection – Machine Vision Lenses and Optical Filters, Specifications and Selection – Imaging Sensors – CCD and CMOS, Specifications – Interface Architectures – Analog and Digital Cameras – Digital Camera Interfaces – Camera Computer Interfaces, Specifications and Selection – Geometrical Image formation models – Camera Calibration

# Scene constraints

Scene constraints refer to the specific limitations or conditions in an environment that affect the quality and accuracy of image acquisition in a machine vision system. These constraints are crucial to consider in designing and implementing machine vision solutions, as they influence how the camera, lighting, and other system components should be configured to capture clear and usable images. Understanding scene constraints helps in selecting the right hardware and optimizing settings to overcome these limitations.

Here are some key scene constraints to consider:

### 1. Lighting Conditions

- **Ambient Lighting:** Variations in natural or artificial ambient lighting can affect image quality, causing reflections, shadows, or inconsistent brightness. For example, a machine vision system near a window may face changing lighting conditions throughout the day, impacting consistency.
- **Controlled Lighting:** To overcome ambient lighting issues, controlled lighting techniques (such as backlighting, ring lights, or diffused lighting) are often used to ensure consistent illumination and highlight relevant features.

### 2. Object Positioning and Orientation

- **Variability in Positioning:** If objects on a conveyor belt are positioned randomly, it becomes challenging for the machine vision system to consistently capture specific features. Positioning constraints require specialized cameras or software algorithms that can detect objects at different angles and positions.
- **Orientation:** Some inspections may need objects in specific orientations. Systems may require fixtures or adjustments to maintain a fixed orientation for accurate imaging or use 3D cameras that can capture features regardless of object orientation.

### 3. Background Conditions

- **Background Complexity:** A complex or cluttered background can interfere with image processing, making it difficult for the system to differentiate between the object and background. Controlled, uniform backgrounds are often used to improve object contrast.
- **Reflective or Textured Surfaces:** Highly reflective or textured backgrounds may create noise or unwanted reflections in the image. Polarizing filters or diffused lighting can help minimize reflections from such surfaces.

### 4. Object Characteristics

- **Color and Texture:** Objects with similar colors or textures may blend into each other, making feature extraction challenging. Selecting specific wavelengths of light (e.g., infrared for darker objects) or using color filters can enhance contrast.
- **Surface Reflectivity:** Highly reflective or shiny surfaces can produce glare, affecting image quality. Adjusting the angle of light or using polarized lighting can reduce glare and improve image clarity.
- **Size and Shape:** The size and shape of objects in a scene impact the choice of camera resolution and lens. Small or detailed objects require higher resolution, while large objects may need multiple cameras or

wider lenses to capture the entire scene.

## 5. Depth of Field (DoF)

- **Object Depth Variation:** If objects vary significantly in depth within the scene, it may cause parts of the object to appear out of focus. Controlling depth of field by adjusting lens aperture or using specialized lenses can help maintain focus across objects at different depths.
- **Focus Requirements:** For applications where features at different depths need inspection, high-depth-of-field lenses, or multifocal imaging, can be used to ensure that all areas of the object remain in focus.

## 6. Motion and Speed of Objects

- **Object Movement:** Fast-moving objects require high-speed cameras with short exposure times to avoid motion blur. The machine vision system must be capable of capturing images at the speed of the moving objects.
- **Vibration:** In industrial settings, vibrations from nearby machines can affect image stability. Using vibration-damping mounts for cameras or strobe lighting (which freezes motion) can reduce these effects.

## 7. Environmental Conditions

- **Temperature and Humidity:** Extreme temperatures or high humidity can impact camera performance, lens clarity, and the stability of other system components. Protective enclosures or cooling systems may be needed in harsh environments.
- **Dust and Contaminants:** Dust, dirt, or oil can accumulate on camera lenses or light sources, obstructing visibility and reducing image quality. Regular maintenance and protective covers can help mitigate this issue.

## 8. Field of View (FoV) Requirements

- **Wide vs. Narrow FoV:** The size of the area to be inspected affects the choice of lenses and camera placement. A wide field of view is needed for large objects or scenes, whereas a narrow field of view is beneficial for detailed inspection.
- **Coverage Constraints:** In some cases, multiple cameras may be required to cover all angles or sides of an object, especially for complex or irregularly shaped objects.

## 9. Contrast and Visibility Constraints

- **Low Contrast:** Objects with low contrast against their background or with subtle features may be difficult to detect. Increasing contrast through specialized lighting or using image enhancement techniques can improve visibility.
- **Color Constraints:** Certain scenes may have specific color requirements to distinguish between object features and background, requiring filters or cameras sensitive to specific color ranges to enhance visibility.

## Summary

Scene constraints encompass the environmental, object, and operational factors that affect image acquisition in a machine vision system. By understanding and managing these constraints—such as lighting, positioning, background, depth of field, movement, and environmental conditions—engineers can design more effective machine vision systems. Proper adjustments, lighting techniques, and equipment selection allow these systems to capture high-quality images, ensuring accurate analysis and reliable performance in real-world industrial applications.

# Lighting Parameters

Lighting parameters are critical considerations in machine vision systems because lighting directly affects the quality, clarity, and contrast of captured images. Proper lighting ensures that the system can detect and analyze features accurately, even in complex or challenging environments. Here's an in-depth look at the key lighting parameters that influence machine vision:

### 1. Intensity (Brightness)

- **Definition:** Intensity refers to the brightness or strength of the light source used in the imaging setup.
- **Importance:** Adequate intensity ensures that all relevant details in an object are visible without shadows or underexposure. Too much intensity can cause glare or overexposure, while insufficient intensity may result in dark, unclear images.
- **Adjustment:** Light intensity can be adjusted to match the reflectivity of the object. For reflective surfaces, lower intensity can reduce glare, while matte surfaces may require higher intensity for proper illumination.

### 2. Color (Wavelength)

- **Definition:** The color of light, or its wavelength, affects how different materials and features appear in an image.
  - **Types:**
- **Visible Light:** Standard white light is commonly used, but different colors (red, blue, green) may help highlight specific features or contrast.
- **Infrared (IR):** Useful for penetrating certain materials or for applications where visible light may be too reflective. IR can reduce glare and enhance contrast.
- **Ultraviolet (UV):** Used to detect surface irregularities, scratches, or certain chemical coatings that fluoresce under UV light.
- **Importance:** Choosing the correct wavelength can significantly improve contrast between object features and the background, enhancing visibility and inspection accuracy.

### 3. Angle and Direction of Illumination

- **Definition:** The angle and direction from which light strikes the object influence the appearance of shadows, reflections, and details in the image.
  - **Types:**
- **Front Lighting:** Illuminates the object directly from the front. Good for capturing surface color and general details.
- **Backlighting:** Places light behind the object, creating a silhouette that highlights edges and contours. Ideal for detecting shapes and dimensions.
- **Side Lighting:** Light from the side emphasizes surface texture, edges, and relief by casting shadows.
- **Ring Lighting:** Uniform, circular lighting around the object minimizes shadows and provides even illumination. Useful for circular or reflective objects.
- **Importance:** The angle and direction of light affect which features are visible and highlighted. For example, side lighting can emphasize textures, while backlighting is effective for identifying edges and silhouettes.

## 4. Lighting Technique

- **Definition:** Different lighting techniques are used to achieve specific effects based on the object's surface characteristics and inspection needs.
  - **Common Techniques:**
- **Diffuse Lighting:** Disperses light evenly, reducing shadows and reflections. Ideal for reflective or shiny surfaces.
- **Structured Lighting:** Projects patterns (like grids or stripes) onto the object to capture 3D information or highlight contours.
  - **Spot Lighting:** Focused light on a specific area to enhance details or highlight particular features.
  - **Dark Field Lighting:** Light directed at a shallow angle illuminates surface flaws, scratches, or edges by creating a high-contrast effect.
- **Importance:** The choice of technique affects the ability to see specific object features clearly, especially for detecting textures, defects, or edges.

## 5. Uniformity

- **Definition:** Uniformity measures how evenly the light is distributed across the scene.
- **Importance:** Non-uniform lighting can lead to variations in image brightness, making it difficult for the system to distinguish between actual object features and lighting inconsistencies.
- **Techniques for Achieving Uniformity:** Diffused lighting and ring lighting setups are often used to ensure consistent illumination across the entire field of view.

## 6. Strobing or Flashing Light

- **Definition:** Strobing refers to using brief, high-intensity flashes of light to freeze motion in high-speed applications.
- **Importance:** Strobe lights are essential for capturing clear images of fast-moving objects without motion blur. They synchronize with the camera's exposure time to provide sharp images.
- **Application:** Common in production lines where objects move rapidly, strobing ensures consistent, high-quality images for inspection and analysis.

## 7. Polarization

- **Definition:** Polarization filters modify light waves to reduce reflections and glare, especially on reflective or shiny surfaces.
  - **Importance:** Polarized lighting enhances the visibility of surface details and reduces unwanted reflections, which is crucial when inspecting glass, metals, or glossy surfaces.
- **Application:** Often used in combination with polarizing filters on cameras to further enhance contrast and reduce glare.

## 8. Coherence

- **Definition:** Coherence refers to the phase relationship between light waves. Lasers, for example, emit coherent light, where all waves are in phase.

- **Importance:** Coherent light (such as laser light) is used in applications requiring precision, like structured lighting for 3D measurements or detecting micro-level surface defects.
- **Application:** In machine vision, coherent lighting can be beneficial for specialized tasks like 3D imaging or surface inspection of tiny features.

### Summary of Lighting Parameters in Machine Vision

Each lighting parameter—intensity, color, angle, technique, uniformity, strobing, polarization, and coherence—plays a vital role in how an object is illuminated and captured in a machine vision system. By adjusting these parameters, engineers can optimize lighting for specific applications, highlighting relevant object features and minimizing visual noise. Proper lighting setup is essential for high-quality imaging, accurate analysis, and reliable performance in machine vision applications across diverse industries.

# Lighting sources

In machine vision systems, selecting the appropriate lighting source is crucial to achieving optimal image quality, contrast, and feature visibility. Different lighting sources offer various characteristics in terms of intensity, color spectrum, longevity, and suitability for specific applications. Here's an overview of the common lighting sources used in machine vision:

## 1. LED (Light Emitting Diode)

- **Characteristics:** LEDs are the most commonly used light source in machine vision. They provide stable, high-intensity light with low heat output and long lifespan. LEDs are available in various colors (visible and non-visible spectrums, including IR and UV) and can be controlled for intensity, pulsing, and strobing.
- **Advantages:** LEDs offer high durability, energy efficiency, and consistent output over time. They are also highly customizable and adaptable to different lighting techniques (e.g., ring lights, bar lights, backlights).
- **Applications:** LEDs are versatile and used in almost all machine vision applications, including quality control, measurement, and defect inspection, due to their reliability and range of configurations.

## 2. Fluorescent Lighting

- **Characteristics:** Fluorescent lights produce diffuse, even illumination, making them suitable for lighting larger areas with moderate intensity. They are available in various color temperatures (warm to cool white) and are relatively inexpensive.
- **Advantages:** Fluorescent lights provide uniform lighting with minimal shadows, making them useful for general-purpose illumination and applications requiring low to moderate brightness.
- **Disadvantages:** Fluorescent lights have a shorter lifespan than LEDs and can flicker, especially as they age. They are also sensitive to temperature changes and may not work well in high-speed or high-precision applications.
- **Applications:** Used for broad, diffused lighting in applications like general inspection or background lighting, where highly controlled lighting isn't necessary.

## 3. Halogen Lighting

- **Characteristics:** Halogen lights produce bright, high-intensity light with a continuous spectrum in the visible range, giving a natural color rendering. However, they generate significant heat and have a shorter lifespan than LEDs.
- **Advantages:** Halogen lights provide bright, warm light, excellent color rendering, and are effective for capturing natural color representations.
- **Disadvantages:** High heat output and relatively short lifespan make them less suitable for prolonged, high-precision applications.
- **Applications:** Used in applications requiring high-intensity lighting with natural color rendering, such as surface inspection and color-based differentiation tasks.

## 4. Xenon Lighting

- **Characteristics:** Xenon lights produce intense, pulsed white light, often used in strobing applications to capture high-speed images. They emit a broad spectrum of light, from UV to infrared, with a very high intensity in short bursts.
- **Advantages:** High-intensity, pulsed light allows for clear images of fast-moving objects by minimizing motion blur. They have high color accuracy and can illuminate objects at greater distances.
- **Disadvantages:** Xenon lights have a limited lifespan, high energy consumption, and may require cooling due to heat generation.
- **Applications:** Common in high-speed machine vision systems, such as those on production lines for fast-moving objects, packaging inspections, and object counting.

### 5. Fiber Optic Lighting

- **Characteristics:** Fiber optic lighting systems channel light from a central source (often a halogen or xenon lamp) through flexible fiber optic cables. These systems provide focused or structured lighting without adding heat near the inspection area.
- **Advantages:** Fiber optics allow for precise, focused lighting and are ideal for small, confined spaces. They enable flexible positioning, providing both spot and structured lighting options.
- **Disadvantages:** Fiber optic systems can be costly, especially when paired with high-intensity light sources.
- **Applications:** Used in applications requiring precise, localized lighting, such as microscopic inspections, detailed part analysis, and when working in tight spaces.

### 6. Laser Lighting

- **Characteristics:** Lasers emit highly coherent, monochromatic light (single wavelength) with a focused beam that can maintain intensity over long distances. They are available in various wavelengths, including visible, IR, and UV.
- **Advantages:** Lasers produce sharp, structured lighting ideal for 3D profiling, depth measurement, and creating high-contrast edges. They are effective in projecting structured light patterns (such as grids or lines) for 3D imaging.
- **Disadvantages:** High initial cost, safety concerns due to laser intensity, and potential risk of overheating with prolonged use.
- **Applications:** Ideal for 3D imaging, surface profiling, defect detection on flat surfaces, and applications requiring precise depth measurement.

### 7. Ultraviolet (UV) Lighting

- **Characteristics:** UV lights emit short-wavelength light outside the visible spectrum. UV lighting reveals features that are not visible under standard lighting, such as certain chemical coatings, biological materials, and surface cracks.
- **Advantages:** UV light can make invisible details visible by causing certain materials to fluoresce. It's especially effective in detecting contaminants, surface damage, and materials with UV-reactive properties.
- **Disadvantages:** Limited applications, and UV lights can cause material degradation over time, so they are generally used in specialized or short-term applications.

- **Applications:** Common in inspection tasks where certain materials or contaminants need to fluoresce, such as in pharmaceutical inspection, counterfeit detection, and crack detection on surfaces.

## 8. Infrared (IR) Lighting

- **Characteristics:** Infrared lighting operates at wavelengths longer than visible light, allowing it to penetrate materials that visible light cannot. IR lighting is particularly effective for reducing glare on reflective surfaces and for imaging through certain materials.
- **Advantages:** IR lighting enhances contrast in low-contrast or high-reflective environments and can be used to inspect materials through some translucent layers.
- **Disadvantages:** Infrared imaging may require specialized cameras and is not suitable for applications where visible color information is required.
- **Applications:** Useful for imaging through certain plastics, viewing through fog or smoke, and inspecting high-gloss or reflective surfaces where visible light might cause glare.

### Summary of Lighting Sources

Each lighting source has distinct characteristics that make it suitable for specific machine vision applications:

- **LED:** Versatile, long-lasting, available in multiple colors and configurations, suitable for general machine vision.
- **Fluorescent:** Provides diffuse, even lighting for broad-area inspection but with limited control and durability.
- **Halogen:** High-intensity, continuous spectrum light for natural color rendering, useful for color-critical applications.
- **Xenon:** Pulsed, high-intensity light for high-speed applications, reducing motion blur.
- **Fiber Optic:** Precise, focused lighting for tight spaces or high-detail inspections.
- **Laser:** Structured light for 3D imaging and depth measurements.
- **UV:** Reveals fluorescent details for detecting surface defects, contaminants, or specific materials.
- **IR:** Reduces glare and penetrates certain materials, useful for high-reflective or translucent surface inspections.

Choosing the right lighting source depends on the application requirements, including object properties, environmental constraints, and specific inspection goals. Proper lighting source selection enhances image quality, ensuring accurate analysis and improved machine vision performance.

# Lighting Techniques

Lighting techniques in machine vision refer to various methods used to illuminate objects in ways that enhance visibility, contrast, and feature detection in images. The goal of these techniques is to optimize image quality by controlling shadows, reflections, glare, and overall illumination so that the system can capture specific details accurately. Choosing the appropriate lighting technique depends on the object's surface characteristics, inspection requirements, and scene constraints.

Here are some commonly used lighting techniques in machine vision:

## 1. Backlighting

- **Description:** Backlighting positions the light source behind the object, creating a silhouette effect. The object appears as a dark shape against a bright background.
- **Benefits:** This technique is ideal for detecting object outlines, edges, and shapes. It enhances contrast and simplifies object separation from the background.
- **Applications:** Used for measuring dimensions, verifying object shapes, detecting holes, and inspecting transparent or translucent objects (e.g., glass bottles or plastic containers).

## 2. Front Lighting

- **Description:** Light is directed from the front, illuminating the object directly from the same side as the camera.
- **Benefits:** Highlights the object's surface color, texture, and details. Front lighting is straightforward and provides good visibility for general inspection.
- **Applications:** Useful for applications where surface details, colors, or markings need to be clearly visible, such as reading labels or detecting surface marks.

## 3. Side Lighting

- **Description:** Side lighting places the light source at an angle to the object, typically from the side.
- **Benefits:** Emphasizes surface texture, raised features, and edges by casting shadows. Side lighting is useful for enhancing contours and detecting small surface imperfections.
- **Applications:** Commonly used in applications where textures, scratches, embossing, or surface relief features are of interest, such as inspecting metal surfaces or embossed patterns.

## 4. Ring Lighting

- **Description:** Ring lighting uses a circular light source placed around the camera lens to provide uniform, shadow-free illumination.
- **Benefits:** Minimizes shadows and provides even lighting, reducing reflections and glare. This technique is effective for capturing details on flat, reflective, or circular objects.
- **Applications:** Ideal for inspecting round or reflective objects, such as inspecting electronic components, circuit boards, or shiny surfaces.

## 5. Diffuse Dome Lighting

- **Description:** Diffuse dome lighting provides soft, even lighting from all angles by surrounding the object with a hemispherical dome that scatters light.
- **Benefits:** Eliminates shadows, reflections, and hot spots, creating uniform illumination across the object's surface.
- **Applications:** Useful for inspecting highly reflective or irregularly shaped objects where reflections and shadows must be minimized, such as inspecting curved surfaces or polished metals.

## 6. Dark Field Lighting

- **Description:** Light is directed at a very shallow angle toward the object's surface, illuminating only raised or recessed features.
- **Benefits:** Creates high contrast between surface imperfections and the background, making scratches, cracks, and other small defects visible.
- **Applications:** Commonly used to inspect glass, lenses, or highly polished surfaces, as well as to detect scratches, cracks, and other fine surface defects.

## 7. Coaxial Lighting

- **Description:** Coaxial lighting involves placing a beam-splitter or mirror above the object to direct light downwards along the camera's optical axis, providing even illumination.
- **Benefits:** Reduces glare and ensures that light reaches only the areas directly beneath the camera. This technique is effective for imaging flat, reflective surfaces without reflections.
- **Applications:** Ideal for inspecting reflective materials, circuit boards, flat surfaces, and detecting surface flaws like solder defects or scratches on metal.

## 8. Structured Lighting

- **Description:** Structured lighting projects a pattern (such as lines, grids, or dots) onto the object's surface, allowing for depth and contour detection.
- **Benefits:** Allows the system to capture 3D information by analyzing how the pattern deforms on the surface. Structured lighting is especially useful for profiling, depth measurement, and contour analysis.
- **Applications:** Used in 3D machine vision applications, such as inspecting complex surfaces, capturing topography, or measuring the depth of objects.

## 9. Polarized Lighting

- **Description:** Polarized lighting uses polarizing filters on both the light source and the camera to reduce glare and reflections from shiny surfaces.
- **Benefits:** Significantly reduces glare and enhances contrast, making it easier to see details on glossy or metallic objects.
- **Applications:** Often used in applications where reflections are problematic, such as inspecting glass, metal, and other shiny materials, or in situations where surfaces need clear differentiation from reflections.

## 10. Low-Angle Lighting

- **Description:** Light is positioned at a low angle relative to the object's surface, similar to dark field lighting, but may be positioned from multiple sides.
- **Benefits:** Enhances the visibility of fine surface details, edges, and textures by casting subtle shadows.
- **Applications:** Suitable for inspecting features like embossed text, engraved markings, and surface textures on flat objects.

### Choosing the Right Lighting Technique

Selecting the correct lighting technique involves understanding the specific inspection needs and object characteristics:

- **Object's Surface Type:** Highly reflective surfaces benefit from diffuse dome lighting or polarized lighting, while textured surfaces benefit from side or low-angle lighting.
- **Feature Type:** Edges, holes, and shapes are best highlighted with backlighting, while surface details require side or dark field lighting.
- **Application Requirements:** For applications requiring 3D measurements, structured lighting is ideal. When working with moving objects, strobing with high-intensity lighting may be required to freeze motion.

### Summary of Lighting Techniques

- **Backlighting:** Enhances edges and silhouettes.
- **Front Lighting:** General illumination for surface features and color.
- **Side Lighting:** Highlights texture and surface details.
- **Ring Lighting:** Provides even, shadow-free lighting.
- **Diffuse Dome Lighting:** Minimizes reflections for uniform lighting.
- **Dark Field Lighting:** Reveals fine surface imperfections.
- **Coaxial Lighting:** Ideal for flat, reflective surfaces.
- **Structured Lighting:** Projects patterns for 3D profiling.
- **Polarized Lighting:** Reduces glare on shiny surfaces.
- **Low-Angle Lighting:** Enhances edges and textures with shallow lighting.

Each lighting technique plays a specific role in optimizing image quality and enhancing certain object features. By carefully selecting the appropriate technique, machine vision systems can achieve clearer, more accurate images tailored to the requirements of industrial inspection, measurement, and quality control applications.

# Machine Vision Lenses and Optical Filters

Machine vision lenses and optical filters are essential components in a machine vision system, as they directly impact the quality, clarity, and accuracy of the images captured. The selection of the right lenses and filters is critical to ensure the system captures the necessary details, enhances contrast, and reduces unwanted artifacts like glare or reflections. Here's an in-depth look at machine vision lenses and optical filters:

## Machine Vision Lenses

Machine vision lenses are specialized optics designed to capture sharp, high-resolution images of objects, often in challenging industrial environments. They differ from regular photographic lenses by offering precise control over focal length, field of view, depth of field, and distortion, which are essential for machine vision applications.

### 1. Types of Machine Vision Lenses

- **Fixed Focal Length (Prime) Lenses:** These lenses have a fixed focal length and offer high image quality and low distortion. They are commonly used when the distance between the camera and the object remains constant.
- **Zoom Lenses:** Zoom lenses have an adjustable focal length, allowing flexibility in the field of view. However, they may introduce more distortion than fixed lenses and are less commonly used in applications requiring high precision.
- **Telecentric Lenses:** Telecentric lenses are designed to eliminate perspective distortion by keeping magnification constant regardless of the object's distance from the lens. This characteristic makes them ideal for precision measurements, as they ensure that objects appear the same size in the image, regardless of depth variation.
- **Wide-Angle Lenses:** These lenses provide a larger field of view, allowing the system to capture a broad scene or large objects at close range. Wide-angle lenses are often used when space is limited but may introduce distortion around the edges.
- **Macro Lenses:** Macro lenses are designed for close-up imaging, capturing small objects or fine details with high magnification. They are ideal for inspecting tiny parts or surface features.
- **Specialty Lenses (e.g., fisheye, bifocal):** Specialty lenses are used in specific applications requiring unique fields of view or specific optical effects, such as panoramic imaging.

### 2. Key Lens Parameters

- **Focal Length:** Determines the magnification and field of view. A shorter focal length provides a wider field of view, while a longer focal length offers higher magnification.
- **Field of View (FoV):** The area visible through the lens at a specific distance. The required FoV depends on the size of the object and the distance between the camera and the object.
- **Depth of Field (DoF):** The range of distances within which the image remains in focus. A larger DoF is essential in applications where the object's height varies or when precise focus across multiple planes is required.
- **Resolution:** Defines the ability of the lens to distinguish fine details. High-resolution lenses are essential for applications requiring detailed inspections, such as defect detection on small parts.

- **Aperture (f-number):** Controls the amount of light entering the lens. A smaller f-number (larger aperture) allows more light, improving performance in low-light conditions, but also reduces depth of field.

### 3. Considerations for Selecting Machine Vision Lenses

- **Object Size and Working Distance:** The lens should provide the appropriate magnification and field of view for the object's size and the distance from the camera.
- **Distortion Requirements:** Some applications require low or no distortion, making telecentric or high-quality fixed focal length lenses preferable.
- **Resolution Needs:** For detailed inspection, select lenses with a resolution matching the camera sensor to capture fine details accurately.
- **Environmental Factors:** For high-vibration environments, choose robust, industrial-grade lenses, and consider protective housings for lenses used in harsh conditions.

### Optical Filters in Machine Vision

Optical filters are used in machine vision systems to control the light reaching the camera sensor, enhancing contrast and selectively highlighting features. Filters help reduce reflections, improve contrast, and eliminate unwanted wavelengths, optimizing image quality for specific applications.

### 1. Types of Optical Filters

- **Polarizing Filters:** These filters reduce reflections and glare from shiny or reflective surfaces by allowing only light waves oscillating in a specific direction to pass through. Polarizers are particularly effective in reducing glare from glass, metals, and glossy surfaces.
- **Color Filters:** Color filters selectively allow certain wavelengths (colors) to pass through while blocking others. For example, a red filter allows red light to pass and blocks other colors. This technique can improve contrast between features or make specific colors stand out.
- **Neutral Density (ND) Filters:** ND filters reduce the overall light intensity without affecting color. They are useful when the scene is too bright, as they prevent overexposure, allowing for better image control.
- **Infrared (IR) and Ultraviolet (UV) Filters:** IR filters block infrared light, allowing only visible light to reach the sensor. UV filters block ultraviolet light, which can cause haze in images. Conversely, IR-pass filters allow only infrared light to pass through, useful for applications requiring IR illumination.
- **Bandpass Filters:** Bandpass filters allow a specific range of wavelengths to pass while blocking all others. This selective filtering is useful in applications where a particular wavelength is needed, such as inspecting colored features or viewing under monochromatic lighting.
- **Longpass and Shortpass Filters:** Longpass filters allow wavelengths longer than a certain cutoff to pass, while shortpass filters allow shorter wavelengths to pass. They are commonly used to separate different spectral regions for targeted inspection.

### 2. Key Considerations for Selecting Optical Filters

- **Application Requirements:** Choose filters based on the specific needs of the application, such as reducing glare, isolating colors, or enhancing contrast.

- **Lighting Conditions:** Select filters that complement the lighting setup. For instance, if the system uses polarized lighting, a polarizing filter on the lens can further enhance glare reduction.
- **Object Characteristics:** If the object has specific colors, reflective properties, or transparency, select filters that highlight these features. For example, a blue filter can help highlight yellow details on an object.
- **Sensor Sensitivity:** Ensure the filter matches the camera's sensitivity range. Some camera sensors are more sensitive to certain wavelengths, so filters should be chosen to optimize image capture within the sensor's capabilities.

### Combined Use of Lenses and Filters

In machine vision systems, lenses and filters are often used together to achieve high-quality images. For example:

- **Telecentric Lens with Polarizing Filter:** Ideal for precise measurement applications involving shiny objects, as it minimizes both perspective distortion and glare.
- **Macro Lens with Bandpass Filter:** Used in close-up inspections of specific colored features or markings, where the bandpass filter highlights the desired color and the macro lens captures fine details.
- **Wide-Angle Lens with IR Filter:** Used in applications requiring a large field of view, while the IR filter enhances contrast on reflective surfaces.

### Summary

Machine vision lenses and optical filters are essential for capturing clear, high-contrast images tailored to the specific needs of industrial applications:

Machine Vision Lenses provide control over magnification, field of view, and depth of field, crucial for applications ranging from detailed inspection to large-scale imaging. Types of lenses, such as telecentric, macro, and wide-angle lenses, offer specific advantages based on application requirements.

Optical Filters control the light reaching the sensor, allowing selective wavelength transmission, glare reduction, and enhanced contrast. Filters like polarizers, color filters, ND filters, and IR/UV filters enable effective imaging under challenging conditions.

By carefully selecting the right combination of lenses and filters, machine vision systems can achieve higher image quality, improved feature detection, and enhanced inspection accuracy across diverse industrial settings.

# Imaging Sensors – CCD and CMOS

Imaging sensors are critical components in machine vision systems, converting light into electrical signals to create digital images. The two primary types of imaging sensors used in machine vision are CCD (Charge-Coupled Device) and CMOS (Complementary Metal-Oxide-Semiconductor) sensors. Each type has unique characteristics, advantages, and limitations that make it suitable for different applications.

## 1. CCD (Charge-Coupled Device) Sensors

CCD sensors were the first to be widely used in digital imaging and have historically been known for producing high-quality images with low noise levels. They work by capturing light in an array of photo-sensitive elements, or pixels, and transferring the electrical charge pixel by pixel across the chip to a readout amplifier, where it's converted to a digital signal.

### Working Principle of CCD Sensors

- Each pixel in a CCD sensor is a small photo-site that converts incoming photons (light particles) into an electrical charge.
- After exposure, the accumulated charges are shifted across the sensor to an output node, where they are read out and digitized.
- This sequential charge transfer produces high-quality images but requires a relatively slow readout process.

### Advantages of CCD Sensors

- **High Image Quality:** CCDs typically produce images with low noise and high sensitivity, making them suitable for applications that require high image quality.
- **Better Light Sensitivity:** CCD sensors are generally more sensitive to light, enabling high-quality imaging in low-light conditions.
- **Uniformity and Consistency:** CCDs offer good uniformity in capturing light, resulting in consistent brightness and color accuracy across the image.

### Limitations of CCD Sensors

- **Power Consumption:** CCD sensors consume more power than CMOS sensors, which can lead to heat generation and shorter battery life in portable applications.
- **Slower Readout Speed:** CCD sensors have slower readout speeds due to the sequential transfer of charges, making them less ideal for high-speed applications.
- **Cost:** Manufacturing CCD sensors is typically more expensive, which can result in higher costs for CCD-based cameras.

### Applications of CCD Sensors

- CCD sensors are ideal for applications where image quality is paramount, and speed is less critical. They are used in fields like scientific imaging, medical imaging, and certain types of industrial inspection that require precise color and image uniformity.

# 2. CMOS (Complementary Metal-Oxide-Semiconductor) Sensors

CMOS sensors are newer than CCDs and have become the dominant technology for most digital cameras, including machine vision applications. CMOS sensors are manufactured using standard semiconductor fabrication processes, which makes them more cost-effective and allows for greater flexibility in design.

## Working Principle of CMOS Sensors

- Each pixel in a CMOS sensor has its own photodetector and amplifier, allowing each pixel to convert light into an electrical charge independently.
- Since each pixel has its own charge-to-voltage conversion circuitry, the sensor can read out pixel data simultaneously, rather than sequentially, resulting in faster data capture and transfer.

## Advantages of CMOS Sensors

- **High Speed:** CMOS sensors allow for faster readout speeds, making them suitable for high-speed applications where rapid imaging is necessary.
- **Lower Power Consumption:** CMOS sensors consume less power than CCD sensors, making them more energy-efficient and suitable for applications where power efficiency is a priority.
- **On-Chip Processing:** CMOS technology allows additional processing capabilities to be integrated directly onto the chip, enabling features such as noise reduction, image correction, and analog-to-digital conversion.
- **Cost-Effective:** CMOS sensors are typically cheaper to manufacture, reducing the overall cost of CMOS-based cameras.

## Limitations of CMOS Sensors

- **Higher Noise Levels:** Although CMOS technology has improved, CMOS sensors can still produce more noise than CCDs, which can affect image quality in low-light situations.
- **Lower Sensitivity:** CMOS sensors generally have lower light sensitivity than CCDs, making them less suitable for low-light applications or applications requiring high dynamic range.
- **Uniformity Challenges:** The independent readout and processing of each pixel can lead to variations in brightness and color across the image, especially in low-light conditions.

## Applications of CMOS Sensors

- CMOS sensors are widely used in applications requiring high-speed imaging, cost-efficiency, or low power consumption, such as automotive imaging, mobile phone cameras, industrial machine vision, and robotics. Their versatility makes them ideal for fast-paced, real-time inspection tasks on production lines.

## Choosing Between CCD and CMOS Sensors in Machine Vision

The choice between CCD and CMOS sensors depends on the specific needs of the application:

- For high-quality imaging where precision, color accuracy, and low noise are essential (such as in scientific imaging or certain types of quality control), CCD sensors may be the preferred choice despite their higher cost and slower readout speed.

- For high-speed imaging and applications where power consumption and cost are critical considerations (such as in real-time industrial inspection or mobile applications), CMOS sensors are typically more suitable.
- **Environmental Conditions:** In high-temperature or harsh environments, CMOS sensors may perform better due to their lower power consumption and heat generation.

## Advances in CMOS Technology

Recent advances in CMOS technology have significantly improved their image quality, light sensitivity, and noise performance, bridging the gap with CCDs for many applications. Modern CMOS sensors now feature:

- **Global Shutter Technology:** Traditional CMOS sensors use a rolling shutter, which can create distortions in fast-moving objects. Newer CMOS sensors with global shutter technology capture the entire image simultaneously, eliminating motion artifacts.
- **Enhanced Light Sensitivity and Noise Reduction:** Advances in pixel architecture and noise reduction techniques have improved the performance of CMOS sensors in low-light conditions.
- **High Dynamic Range (HDR):** Many CMOS sensors now offer HDR capabilities, capturing more detail in scenes with a wide range of brightness levels, which is valuable in industrial environments with variable lighting.

## Summary

CCD Sensors offer high image quality, better light sensitivity, and uniformity, making them ideal for applications where image accuracy is critical and speed is less important.

CMOS Sensors provide faster readout speeds, lower power consumption, and lower cost, making them more suitable for high-speed, real-time applications and environments where cost efficiency is essential.

Both CCD and CMOS sensors have distinct advantages and limitations. The choice depends on the balance between image quality, speed, power consumption, and cost required by the application, with CMOS sensors now being the dominant choice for most industrial machine vision applications due to their versatility and continuous technological improvements.

# CCD and CMOS - Specifications

CCD (Charge-Coupled Device) and CMOS (Complementary Metal-Oxide-Semiconductor) sensors have various specifications that impact their performance and suitability for different machine vision applications. Understanding these specifications helps in selecting the appropriate sensor type based on the requirements of image quality, speed, sensitivity, power consumption, and cost.

Here's an overview of the key specifications of CCD and CMOS sensors and how they differ:

## 1. Resolution

- **Definition:** Resolution is the number of pixels in the sensor, typically represented as the width by height (e.g., 1920x1080). Higher resolution allows for more detailed images and better feature detection.
- **CCD:** Often chosen for high-resolution imaging, particularly in applications requiring high-quality and noise-free images. CCD sensors tend to offer excellent image sharpness due to uniform pixel structure.
- **CMOS:** CMOS sensors also offer high resolutions, especially as technology has improved. They are widely used in applications requiring high resolution and high-speed imaging, like real-time inspection.
- **Applications:** High-resolution sensors are necessary in detailed inspection tasks (e.g., defect detection, micro-inspection) and quality control.

## 2. Pixel Size

- **Definition:** Pixel size is the physical size of each pixel on the sensor, usually measured in micrometers ($\mu$m). Larger pixels can capture more light, improving sensitivity and reducing noise.
- **CCD:** CCD sensors traditionally have larger pixel sizes, making them more sensitive to light and ideal for low-light conditions.
- **CMOS:** CMOS sensors are available in a range of pixel sizes, with smaller pixels becoming common in high-resolution applications. Smaller pixels can result in higher noise, but modern CMOS sensors mitigate this with advanced noise reduction.
- **Applications:** Large pixel sizes are beneficial in low-light applications, such as night vision or dimly lit production environments. Smaller pixel sizes are useful in high-resolution applications where lighting conditions are well-controlled.

## 3. Dynamic Range

- **Definition:** Dynamic range is the range of light intensities that the sensor can capture, from the darkest to the brightest parts. Higher dynamic range allows sensors to capture more details in scenes with high contrast.
- **CCD:** Generally, CCD sensors offer a high dynamic range, making them suitable for capturing details in both dark and bright areas.
- **CMOS:** CMOS sensors have improved significantly in dynamic range and can now offer comparable performance, especially with High Dynamic Range (HDR) capabilities.
- **Applications:** High dynamic range is essential for environments with variable lighting or scenes with significant contrast, such as outdoor inspection or imaging objects with reflective and shadowed areas.

## 4. Sensitivity

- **Definition:** Sensitivity measures how well a sensor can capture light, especially in low-light conditions. Higher sensitivity means that less light is needed to achieve a clear image.
- **CCD:** CCD sensors have historically been more sensitive to light due to their larger pixels and low noise characteristics, making them ideal for low-light imaging.
- **CMOS:** While early CMOS sensors had lower sensitivity, advancements in technology have improved CMOS sensitivity, making it suitable for various lighting conditions.
- **Applications:** High sensitivity is required in low-light applications such as medical imaging, night-time inspections, and dimly lit industrial settings.

### 5. Signal-to-Noise Ratio (SNR)

- **Definition:** SNR is the ratio of the signal (useful light) to noise (unwanted variations), with higher SNR indicating cleaner images.
- **CCD:** CCD sensors typically have a higher SNR, resulting in lower noise and clearer images, especially in low-light conditions.
- **CMOS:** CMOS sensors may have a lower SNR, but advancements in noise reduction technology have closed the gap with CCD sensors, making them viable in applications that require high image quality.
- **Applications:** High SNR is critical for applications needing detailed image clarity, such as quality inspection, microscopy, and defect detection.

### 6. Shutter Type

- **Definition:** Shutter type determines how the sensor captures the image. Global shutter captures the entire image at once, while rolling shutter captures the image line by line.
- **CCD:** CCD sensors use a global shutter, which eliminates motion artifacts and is essential for high-precision applications.
- **CMOS:** CMOS sensors typically use a rolling shutter, though many modern CMOS sensors now include global shutter options to avoid distortions in high-speed imaging.
- **Applications:** A global shutter is ideal for high-speed, precision applications where objects move quickly, such as production line inspection and high-speed counting.

### 7. Frame Rate

- **Definition:** Frame rate is the number of frames captured per second (fps). Higher frame rates are essential for real-time or high-speed applications.
- **CCD:** CCD sensors generally have slower frame rates due to sequential charge transfer, making them less ideal for high-speed applications.
- **CMOS:** CMOS sensors are capable of much higher frame rates due to their parallel readout, making them ideal for real-time, high-speed applications.
- **Applications:** High frame rates are critical for applications like real-time inspection, high-speed assembly line monitoring, and robotics.

### 8. Power Consumption

- **Definition:** Power consumption refers to the amount of power a sensor requires to operate. Lower power consumption helps reduce heat generation and energy costs.

- **CCD:** CCD sensors typically consume more power than CMOS sensors, generating more heat.
- **CMOS:** CMOS sensors have lower power consumption, making them more suitable for applications with limited power availability or where heat generation is a concern.
- **Applications:** Low-power consumption is advantageous in mobile or remote applications, such as drones, robotic vision, and portable inspection devices.

## 9. Cost

- **Definition:** Cost refers to the expense of the sensor and is influenced by factors like sensor complexity, size, and production method.
- **CCD:** CCD sensors are generally more expensive due to their manufacturing process and high-quality image output.
- **CMOS:** CMOS sensors are typically more cost-effective to produce, especially in large volumes, due to the standard semiconductor fabrication process.
- **Applications:** Cost considerations are essential in high-volume or budget-sensitive applications, where CMOS sensors are often preferred.

### Choosing Between CCD and CMOS Sensors

- **High-Resolution and High-Quality Applications:** If high resolution and low noise are essential, CCD sensors may be preferred, especially for scientific imaging, high-precision measurements, and medical imaging.
- **High-Speed and Real-Time Applications:** For applications requiring high frame rates and low power consumption, CMOS sensors are more suitable. They are commonly used in industrial inspection, robotics, and automotive applications.
- **Low-Light Conditions:** CCD sensors have historically been better for low-light applications due to their sensitivity and higher SNR, but recent CMOS advancements offer viable alternatives with improved sensitivity and noise performance.
- **Cost-Sensitive Applications:** CMOS sensors are generally more affordable and are widely used in high-volume applications where budget constraints are critical.

In summary, CCD and CMOS sensors each have specifications that suit different applications. CCD sensors are often chosen for their image quality and light sensitivity, while CMOS sensors are preferred for high-speed, low-power, and cost-sensitive applications. The choice between CCD and CMOS depends on the specific requirements of the machine vision task at hand, including resolution, speed, sensitivity, power consumption, and cost.

# CCD and CMOS – Interface Architectures

CCD (Charge-Coupled Device) and CMOS (Complementary Metal-Oxide-Semiconductor) sensors rely on different interface architectures to transfer the captured image data to the camera system or a connected device for processing. The interface architecture affects how quickly and efficiently image data is transmitted, as well as the power consumption, complexity, and speed of the overall machine vision system.

Here's an in-depth look at CCD and CMOS interface architectures and how they differ:

## 1. CCD Interface Architecture

CCD sensors capture and transfer data using a serial charge-transfer process that shifts the charge through the sensor pixel by pixel. This architecture is based on the bucket-brigade principle, where each pixel acts like a bucket, transferring its charge to the adjacent pixel until the entire row or column reaches the output amplifier.

### Key Components of CCD Interface Architecture

- **Pixel Array:** An array of photosensitive elements (pixels) collects and stores light as electrical charge.
- **Serial Charge Transfer:** Each pixel's charge is transferred in a sequential manner across the array. The charges are moved to a single output node (or multiple nodes in advanced CCDs).
- **Output Amplifier:** The output amplifier converts the accumulated charge into a voltage signal for each pixel, which is then digitized and read out.
- **Timing Controller:** This unit synchronizes the sequential charge transfer process, ensuring that data is read out in the correct order.

### Characteristics of CCD Interface Architecture

- **Sequential Readout:** The pixel data is transferred pixel by pixel, resulting in slower readout speeds compared to CMOS. The sequential process is also power-intensive, leading to higher energy consumption.
- **High-Quality Output:** Due to the uniform charge transfer process and dedicated readout path, CCD sensors are known for low noise and high image quality. They deliver consistent and even data across the sensor.
- **Global Shutter Operation:** CCDs typically use a global shutter, meaning all pixels capture the light simultaneously and are read out together. This avoids motion artifacts and distortion.

### Advantages of CCD Interface Architecture

- **Image Quality:** CCD architecture minimizes noise and produces high-quality images with uniform brightness and color.
- **Low Noise:** The single output channel reduces noise levels, making CCDs ideal for low-light and high-precision applications.

### Limitations of CCD Interface Architecture

- **Slower Readout Speed:** The sequential charge transfer process limits readout speed, making CCDs less suitable for high-speed applications.
- **Higher Power Consumption:** CCDs consume more power than CMOS sensors due to the charge transfer process and the global shutter, resulting in heat generation.

### Applications of CCD Interface Architecture

- CCD sensors are suitable for applications requiring high image quality, low noise, and low-light performance, such as scientific imaging, astronomy, and certain types of medical and industrial inspection.

### 2. CMOS Interface Architecture

CMOS sensors use a parallel, on-chip processing approach that allows each pixel to convert light to a digital signal independently. Each pixel has its own photodetector and amplifier, enabling simultaneous readout from multiple pixels. This architecture allows CMOS sensors to achieve faster readout speeds and reduced power consumption compared to CCDs.

### Key Components of CMOS Interface Architecture

- **Pixel Array with Photodiodes:** Each pixel has a photodiode that converts light into an electrical charge. Each pixel also has its own amplifier and analog-to-digital converter (ADC).
- **Parallel Data Readout:** CMOS sensors read out data in parallel, which means each row (or column) can be read simultaneously, allowing much faster data transfer.
- **On-Chip Processing:** CMOS sensors integrate additional processing circuitry, such as amplifiers and ADCs, directly onto the sensor chip. This allows data to be digitized at the pixel level.
- **Rolling or Global Shutter:** CMOS sensors traditionally use a rolling shutter, where rows are exposed sequentially, though many modern CMOS sensors also offer global shutter options for distortion-free imaging.

### Characteristics of CMOS Interface Architecture

- **High-Speed Readout:** The parallel readout capability allows for much faster image data transfer than CCD sensors, making CMOS sensors suitable for high-speed imaging.
- **Lower Power Consumption:** CMOS sensors consume less power because each pixel has its own readout circuitry, and there's no need to transfer charges across the sensor.
- **Flexibility in Functionality:** CMOS architecture allows for additional functionalities like on-chip noise reduction, high dynamic range (HDR), and low-light optimization, enhancing the sensor's versatility.

### Advantages of CMOS Interface Architecture

- **Faster Frame Rates:** The parallel readout allows for high frame rates, essential for real-time and high-speed applications.
- **Power Efficiency:** Lower power consumption makes CMOS sensors ideal for portable, mobile, and battery-operated devices.

- **Integration Capabilities:** On-chip processing allows for extra features like noise reduction, HDR, and digital processing directly on the sensor.

## Limitations of CMOS Interface Architecture

- **Rolling Shutter Artifacts:** Rolling shutters can cause motion artifacts, though this has been addressed in newer global shutter CMOS designs.
- **Higher Noise:** Due to individual readout circuits at each pixel, CMOS sensors can be more prone to noise, though modern CMOS technology has improved noise reduction significantly.

## Applications of CMOS Interface Architecture

- CMOS sensors are widely used in applications requiring high-speed, real-time imaging, such as industrial automation, robotics, automotive imaging, and mobile devices. Their low power consumption and high frame rates make them ideal for dynamic environments.

## Choosing Between CCD and CMOS Interface Architectures

The choice between CCD and CMOS interface architectures largely depends on the application requirements:

- **High-Speed Applications:** For applications needing high frame rates and low latency, CMOS sensors are ideal due to their parallel readout architecture.
- **Power-Constrained Applications:** CMOS sensors, with their lower power consumption, are preferable for portable, mobile, or battery-operated systems.
- **High Image Quality:** CCD sensors are still preferred for applications where high image quality, low noise, and consistent brightness are paramount, such as scientific or low-light imaging.
- **Cost Sensitivity:** CMOS sensors are generally more cost-effective and scalable, making them suitable for high-volume applications like consumer electronics, automotive imaging, and industrial automation.

## Summary

**CCD Interface Architecture:** Sequential charge transfer with a global shutter, offering high image quality, low noise, but slower readout speed and higher power consumption.

**CMOS Interface Architecture:** Parallel data readout with per-pixel processing, offering high-speed readout, lower power consumption, and on-chip processing capabilities but with potential for rolling shutter artifacts.

Each architecture has unique advantages and limitations. CCD interface architectures are suited for precision and low-light imaging, while CMOS architectures provide speed, efficiency, and advanced integration, making them the preferred choice for most high-speed and real-time machine vision applications.

# Analog and Digital Cameras

Analog and Digital Cameras are two fundamental types of cameras used in imaging and machine vision. They differ primarily in how they capture, process, and transmit image data. Understanding these differences is crucial when selecting the appropriate camera type for specific machine vision applications.

## 1. Analog Cameras

- Analog cameras are traditional imaging devices that convert captured images into continuous analog signals. They transmit image data in real-time via coaxial cables or other analog transmission media to a display monitor or analog-to-digital converter (ADC) for digitization.

### Characteristics of Analog Cameras

- **Signal Transmission:** Analog cameras produce a continuous electrical signal representing light intensity and color information. This signal is usually transmitted using composite video (e.g., NTSC, PAL) or S-Video standards.
- **Real-Time Output:** Analog cameras provide real-time image data without buffering or latency, which can be advantageous in applications needing immediate visual feedback.
- **Resolution and Quality:** Analog cameras typically offer lower resolution and image quality than digital cameras, as the continuous signal format limits fine detail capture.
- **Compatibility:** Analog cameras require specific monitors, video capture cards, or analog-to-digital converters to display and digitize images, making them less flexible than digital cameras in modern setups.

### Advantages of Analog Cameras

- **Low Latency:** Since analog cameras transmit a continuous signal, there's minimal latency, making them suitable for real-time visual feedback.
- **Cost-Effective:** Analog cameras are often cheaper than digital cameras, particularly in setups where high resolution and advanced processing are not required.
- **Simple Setup:** These cameras typically have straightforward connectivity, making them easy to install in systems where legacy analog video systems are still in use.

### Limitations of Analog Cameras

- **Lower Resolution:** Analog cameras are generally limited in resolution, usually maxing out at around 576i (PAL) or 480i (NTSC), making them less ideal for applications requiring high detail.
- **Signal Degradation:** The quality of the signal can degrade over longer cable distances or due to interference, leading to reduced image clarity and reliability.
- **Limited Compatibility with Modern Systems:** Most modern machine vision systems and processing software are optimized for digital inputs, so analog cameras often need conversion equipment to be compatible.

### Applications of Analog Cameras

- Analog cameras are typically used in legacy systems, basic monitoring tasks, and applications where real-time feedback is essential but high image quality is not. Examples include basic security surveillance, simple monitoring, and older industrial setups.

## 2. Digital Cameras

- Digital cameras capture images as digital data, storing pixel information as binary values. This digital data can be easily processed, stored, and transmitted to computers for analysis, making digital cameras highly compatible with modern machine vision systems.

### Characteristics of Digital Cameras

- **Signal Transmission:** Digital cameras transmit data in digital formats over interfaces such as USB, Ethernet, GigE (Gigabit Ethernet), FireWire, Camera Link, and CoaXPress.
- **Image Resolution and Quality:** Digital cameras offer high-resolution options, often supporting megapixel or higher resolutions, which allows for detailed image capture and processing.
- **Processing Capability:** Digital cameras often incorporate advanced features like on-camera image processing, noise reduction, and high-dynamic-range (HDR) imaging, enhancing image quality and flexibility.
- **Data Format:** Digital data is easier to store, transmit, and manipulate without quality loss, allowing for high precision and consistent image quality across multiple use cases.

### Advantages of Digital Cameras

- **High Resolution:** Digital cameras provide high-resolution imaging, often in the megapixel range, making them suitable for applications needing detailed images.
- **Better Image Quality:** Digital cameras can capture images with higher dynamic range and less noise, especially when combined with advanced processing features.
- **Advanced Compatibility and Flexibility:** Digital cameras are compatible with modern computers, software, and machine vision systems, allowing easy integration and scalability.
- **Long-Distance Transmission:** With digital interfaces, data can be transmitted over long distances without quality degradation, which is beneficial for large or distributed systems.

### Limitations of Digital Cameras

- **Higher Latency:** Digital cameras may introduce some latency due to data processing and buffering, although this can be minimized with high-speed interfaces and optimized software.
- **Higher Cost:** Digital cameras are typically more expensive than analog cameras, especially high-resolution models with advanced features.
- **Complexity in Setup:** The initial setup may be more complex, requiring specific software, drivers, and interface configuration, particularly in high-speed applications.

### Applications of Digital Cameras

- Digital cameras are widely used in modern machine vision systems, robotics, automation, and industries requiring detailed image capture and advanced processing capabilities. Applications include quality control, high-resolution inspection, 3D imaging, barcode reading, and detailed visual analysis in fields like electronics, pharmaceuticals, and automotive manufacturing.

## Choosing Between Analog and Digital Cameras

The choice between analog and digital cameras largely depends on the specific application requirements:

- For high-resolution imaging and advanced processing needs, digital cameras are the best choice. They offer greater flexibility, compatibility with modern systems, and high-quality imaging suitable for inspection, automation, and quality control.
- For basic or real-time monitoring in legacy systems, analog cameras may be more cost-effective and simpler to implement. They are suitable for applications where detailed imaging isn't critical, but immediate visual feedback is essential.

## Interface Options for Digital Cameras

Digital cameras use a range of interfaces that allow flexibility in terms of speed, distance, and compatibility:

- **USB:** Common in consumer and some industrial applications, USB is easy to use but limited in speed and distance.
- **GigE (Gigabit Ethernet):** Allows high-speed data transfer over long distances (up to 100 meters), ideal for networked systems.
- **FireWire:** Older interface still in use for some industrial cameras, offering reliable speed for mid-range applications.
- **Camera Link:** High-speed, low-latency interface often used in high-performance machine vision applications.
- **CoaXPress:** High-speed interface capable of handling ultra-high-resolution and high-frame-rate imaging, often used in demanding machine vision tasks.

## Summary

**Analog Cameras:** Analog cameras transmit images as continuous signals. They offer low latency and cost-effectiveness but have limited resolution and are prone to signal degradation. They are suitable for basic monitoring, legacy systems, and applications where real-time visual feedback is prioritized over image quality.

**Digital Cameras:** Digital cameras capture images as digital data, providing high resolution, advanced processing capabilities, and reliable long-distance data transmission. Digital cameras are highly compatible with modern machine vision systems and are used for high-precision tasks, high-speed applications, and environments where detailed inspection is required.

Digital cameras are now the preferred choice in most machine vision applications due to their flexibility, high image quality, and compatibility with advanced processing techniques, while analog cameras remain viable for specific low-cost, real-time visual monitoring setups.

# Digital Camera Interfaces

Digital camera interfaces are the communication protocols and physical connections used to transfer image data from a digital camera to a computer or processing unit in a machine vision system. These interfaces determine the speed, data bandwidth, cable length, power delivery, and overall system complexity, making it essential to choose the right interface based on application requirements. Here's a breakdown of the most common digital camera interfaces used in machine vision:

## 1. USB (Universal Serial Bus)

USB is one of the most widely used interfaces for digital cameras due to its simplicity, wide compatibility, and plug-and-play functionality.

### Characteristics of USB Interface

- **Versions:** The common USB standards are USB 2.0, USB 3.0, USB 3.1, and USB 3.2, each offering progressively faster speeds.
- **USB 2.0:** Up to 480 Mbps (60 MB/s) - suitable for lower-resolution or moderate frame rate applications.
- **USB 3.0 and USB 3.1:** Up to 5 Gbps (625 MB/s) - allows for high-resolution and high-frame-rate imaging.
- **USB 3.2:** Up to 20 Gbps (2.5 GB/s) - suitable for very high data-intensive applications.
- **Cable Length:** USB is typically limited to around 5 meters (USB 2.0), though USB 3.0 and higher can extend up to 3 meters for reliable data transmission. Active or repeater cables can extend this range but may introduce latency.
- **Power Delivery:** USB provides power through the same cable, simplifying setup by eliminating the need for an external power source.
- **Plug-and-Play:** USB cameras are easy to install and widely compatible with computers and industrial systems, making them ideal for flexible applications.

### Applications of USB Interface

USB is ideal for applications requiring portability, simplicity, and moderate to high data rates, such as general inspection, laboratory imaging, and moderate-speed industrial tasks.

## 2. GigE (Gigabit Ethernet)

Gigabit Ethernet, commonly referred to as GigE, is a widely adopted camera interface in industrial environments due to its ability to transmit data over long distances.

### Characteristics of GigE Interface

- **Speed:** Standard GigE offers data rates up to 1 Gbps (125 MB/s). The GigE Vision standard allows cameras to work over Ethernet networks in machine vision applications.
- **Extended Range:** GigE supports cable lengths up to 100 meters with standard Ethernet cables (Cat5e or Cat6), making it suitable for large or distributed systems.
- **Power-over-Ethernet (PoE):** Many GigE cameras support PoE, allowing them to receive power and transmit data through a single Ethernet cable, simplifying installations.

- **Networking Capabilities:** Multiple GigE cameras can connect to a single computer via a network switch, enabling complex setups with multiple cameras.

## Applications of GigE Interface

GigE is ideal for distributed systems, large factory floors, and applications requiring multiple cameras in different locations, such as surveillance, automotive inspection, and quality control in industrial automation.

### 3. 10 GigE (10 Gigabit Ethernet)

10 GigE is an extension of the GigE interface, providing significantly higher bandwidth for applications with intensive data requirements.

## Characteristics of 10 GigE Interface

- **Speed:** 10 Gbps (1.25 GB/s), enabling high-resolution, high-frame-rate imaging with minimal latency.
- **Cable Length:** Supports up to 100 meters with fiber-optic cables or up to 30 meters with copper cables.
- **Low Latency:** The increased bandwidth allows for low-latency data transfer, making 10 GigE suitable for applications requiring rapid data processing.
- **High Power Requirements:** 10 GigE interfaces typically require more power than standard GigE, sometimes necessitating additional cooling in high-speed systems.

## Applications of 10 GigE Interface

10 GigE is commonly used in applications requiring ultra-high-resolution imaging, high-speed processing, and minimal latency, such as semiconductor inspection, medical imaging, and scientific research.

### 4. Camera Link

Camera Link is a high-speed interface developed specifically for machine vision applications, offering robust data transmission with minimal latency.

## Characteristics of Camera Link Interface

- **Speed:** Supports data rates ranging from 255 MB/s (Base configuration) up to 850 MB/s (Full configuration).
- **Cable Length:** Limited to around 10 meters for reliable performance, though active repeaters can extend this range slightly.
- **Real-Time Data Transfer:** Camera Link operates with very low latency, making it ideal for high-speed, high-precision applications.
- **Separate Power Supply:** Most Camera Link cameras require an external power source as the interface does not provide power.

## Applications of Camera Link Interface

Camera Link is ideal for high-performance, low-latency applications that require high frame rates and large amounts of data, such as 3D imaging, real-time inspection, and motion analysis.

## 5. CoaXPress (CXP)

CoaXPress (CXP) is a high-speed interface designed for professional and industrial machine vision, combining high data rates, long cable lengths, and real-time data transfer.

### Characteristics of CoaXPress Interface

- **Speed:** Offers data rates up to 6.25 Gbps per cable, with up to 25 Gbps achievable with multiple cables.
- **Cable Length:** Supports up to 40 meters at high speeds (6.25 Gbps) or up to 100 meters at lower speeds, using coaxial cables.
- **Power and Data Over Single Cable:** CoaXPress supports power delivery over the same cable, reducing cable clutter and simplifying installations.
- **Compatibility with High-Resolution Imaging:** CoaXPress is optimized for high-resolution and high-speed applications, offering real-time, low-latency performance.

### Applications of CoaXPress Interface

CoaXPress is used in demanding applications requiring high-speed, high-resolution data transfer, such as industrial inspection, aerospace, defense, and scientific imaging.

## 6. FireWire (IEEE 1394)

FireWire, also known as IEEE 1394, was a popular interface for digital cameras before the rise of USB 3.0 and GigE. It is still used in some legacy systems and certain industrial applications.

### Characteristics of FireWire Interface

- **Versions:** FireWire 400 (400 Mbps) and FireWire 800 (800 Mbps), both offering moderate data rates.
- **Cable Length:** Typically supports up to 4.5 meters, though FireWire repeaters can extend this range.
- **Peer-to-Peer Communication:** FireWire supports peer-to-peer communication, allowing multiple cameras to connect without needing a central computer.
- **Data and Power Over Single Cable:** FireWire cameras can receive both data and power over the same cable, simplifying connections.

### Applications of FireWire Interface

FireWire is suitable for applications that require moderate data rates, such as legacy systems, certain industrial tasks, and specialized setups that already use FireWire infrastructure.

## 7. HD-SDI (High-Definition Serial Digital Interface)

HD-SDI is a standard used in broadcasting and some industrial applications to transmit uncompressed, high-definition video over coaxial cables.

### Characteristics of HD-SDI Interface

- **Speed:** Transmits uncompressed video up to 3 Gbps, supporting high-definition video.

- **Cable Length:** Generally limited to around 100 meters for HD-SDI, although longer distances can be achieved with repeaters.
- **Low Latency:** HD-SDI offers real-time, low-latency transmission suitable for monitoring applications.
- **No Power Over Cable:** HD-SDI requires a separate power source as it does not provide power to the camera.

### Applications of HD-SDI Interface

HD-SDI is commonly used in broadcast and surveillance applications where uncompressed video and low latency are required. It is less common in industrial machine vision due to limited data rate and integration options.

### Choosing the Right Interface

- **High-Speed, High-Resolution Applications:** CoaXPress and 10 GigE are ideal for applications requiring ultra-fast data transfer, minimal latency, and long distances, such as semiconductor inspection or high-speed quality control.
- **Moderate-Speed Industrial Applications:** GigE is a flexible choice for distributed systems and multi-camera setups, providing reliable data transfer over long distances.
- **Compact, Portable Systems:** USB cameras are ideal for applications requiring easy setup, portability, and lower data rates, such as lab-based inspections.
- **Real-Time, Low-Latency Requirements:** Camera Link and HD-SDI offer low latency for real-time applications, though Camera Link is better suited to machine vision applications due to its higher data throughput.

Choosing the right digital camera interface depends on factors like data speed, distance, power delivery, and specific application requirements.

# Camera Computer Interfaces

Camera-computer interfaces in machine vision are the communication protocols and physical connections used to transfer image data from a camera to a computer or processing unit. The choice of interface is critical, as it affects data transfer speed, latency, cable length, power delivery, and overall system performance. Each interface is suited to specific application requirements based on the bandwidth, distance, and speed required. Below is an overview of the key camera-computer interfaces used in machine vision.

## 1. USB (Universal Serial Bus)

USB is one of the most widely used interfaces for digital cameras in machine vision due to its ease of use, compatibility, and plug-and-play functionality.

### Specifications:

- **Versions:** USB 2.0 (480 Mbps), USB 3.0 (5 Gbps), USB 3.1/3.2 (up to 20 Gbps).
- **Cable Length:** USB 2.0 is reliable up to 5 meters, while USB 3.0 and higher are typically effective up to 3 meters. Active cables or repeaters can extend these distances.
- **Power Delivery:** USB provides power through the same cable, which simplifies setup.
- **Applications:** USB is suitable for lab imaging, moderate-speed inspections, and portable setups where cable length isn't an issue.

## 2. GigE (Gigabit Ethernet)

Gigabit Ethernet, commonly known as GigE, is widely adopted for industrial applications because it allows long cable lengths and networked configurations.

### Specifications:

- **Speed:** GigE transmits at 1 Gbps, and the GigE Vision standard allows easy integration into industrial systems.
- **Cable Length:** GigE cables can extend up to 100 meters using Cat5e or Cat6 Ethernet cables.
- **Power-over-Ethernet (PoE):** Many GigE cameras support PoE, which supplies power and data through a single cable.
- **Applications:** GigE is ideal for large-scale factory setups, distributed systems, and applications where multiple cameras are networked together.

## 3. 10 GigE (10 Gigabit Ethernet)

An upgrade of the GigE interface, 10 GigE provides a significant bandwidth increase for data-intensive applications.

### Specifications:

- **Speed:** 10 Gbps, enabling very high-speed data transfer for high-resolution and high-frame-rate imaging.
- **Cable Length:** Fiber optic cables can support up to 100 meters, and copper cables work for shorter distances up to around 30 meters.

- **Power Requirements:** 10 GigE does not support PoE, requiring external power.
- **Applications:** 10 GigE is suitable for ultra-high-resolution, high-speed applications, such as semiconductor inspection and scientific research.

## 4. Camera Link

Camera Link is a high-speed interface specifically designed for machine vision, offering fast, low-latency data transmission.

### Specifications:

- **Speed:** Data rates range from 255 MB/s (Base configuration) to 850 MB/s (Full configuration).
- **Cable Length:** Typically up to 10 meters; repeaters can slightly extend this distance.
- **Power Delivery:** Camera Link does not support power delivery; an external power supply is required.
- **Applications:** Camera Link is ideal for applications needing high frame rates and low latency, such as high-speed inspection, real-time processing, and motion capture.

## 5. CoaXPress (CXP)

CoaXPress (CXP) is a high-speed interface used in professional and industrial machine vision, designed for data-intensive and high-resolution applications.

### Specifications:

- **Speed:** Up to 6.25 Gbps per channel, scalable to 25 Gbps with multiple channels.
- **Cable Length:** Supports up to 40 meters at full speed (6.25 Gbps) and up to 100 meters at lower speeds.
- **Power Over Cable:** CXP allows power delivery over the same cable, reducing the need for additional cables.
- **Applications:** CoaXPress is used in applications requiring high data throughput and low latency, such as high-speed quality control, aerospace, and scientific imaging.

## 6. FireWire (IEEE 1394)

FireWire, also known as IEEE 1394, was a popular interface for digital cameras but has become less common due to advancements in USB and Ethernet. It is still used in some legacy systems.

### Specifications:

- **Versions:** FireWire 400 (400 Mbps) and FireWire 800 (800 Mbps).
- **Cable Length:** Supports up to 4.5 meters, with repeaters extending this range.
- **Power Delivery:** FireWire can deliver power over the same cable.
- **Applications:** FireWire is used in legacy systems and specific industrial setups where FireWire infrastructure is already established.

## 7. HD-SDI (High-Definition Serial Digital Interface)

HD-SDI is commonly used in broadcast applications and some industrial applications that require uncompressed video transmission.

## Specifications:

- **Speed:** Up to 3 Gbps, supporting high-definition video transmission.
- **Cable Length:** Effective up to 100 meters over coaxial cables.
- **Power Requirements:** HD-SDI does not deliver power; an external power source is needed.
- **Applications:** HD-SDI is typically used for live monitoring and broadcasting, with less common use in machine vision due to limited integration options.

## Key Factors in Interface Selection

When selecting a camera-computer interface, consider the following specifications:

### Data Rate (Bandwidth)

- The required data rate depends on the image resolution, color depth, and frame rate. Interfaces like USB 3.0, GigE, Camera Link, and CoaXPress provide high bandwidth suitable for detailed and high-speed imaging.

### Cable Length

- Cable length requirements vary with application layout. GigE and CoaXPress support longer cable lengths up to 100 meters, ideal for large-scale installations. USB and Camera Link are more suited for shorter distances, around 3-10 meters.

### Power Delivery

- Interfaces such as USB, PoE-enabled GigE, and CoaXPress can deliver power directly through the data cable, simplifying setup. This is particularly useful for distributed and remote installations.

### Latency and Real-Time Processing

- For applications requiring low latency and real-time processing, interfaces like Camera Link and CoaXPress are suitable due to their high-speed, low-latency data transmission. GigE and 10 GigE may also work well, but additional network latency may need consideration.

### Multi-Camera Support

- In applications where multiple cameras are used, GigE and USB interfaces allow for straightforward integration, often with support for multiple cameras connected through a network or hub.

### Environmental Suitability

- Harsh industrial environments may require ruggedized cables and connectors. GigE and CoaXPress are known for durability and resilience, while USB may be less robust in harsh settings.

## Choosing the Right Interface

For high-speed and high-resolution applications like semiconductor inspection, scientific imaging, or high-speed quality control, CoaXPress, 10 GigE, or Camera Link are recommended due to their high data rates and low latency.

For large or distributed systems, GigE or 10 GigE are preferred, offering long cable lengths and easy networking capabilities for multiple-camera setups.

For real-time, low-latency applications requiring minimal delay, Camera Link and CoaXPress are well-suited due to their low-latency transfer.

For basic, budget-conscious applications needing moderate data rates, USB provides ease of use, widespread compatibility, and plug-and-play functionality.

In summary, the choice of camera-computer interface depends on the application's data rate, distance, power needs, and cost considerations. Selecting the right interface ensures reliable and efficient data transfer, enabling optimal performance for machine vision applications.

# Geometrical Image Formation Models

Geometrical image formation models are mathematical models that describe how images are formed in cameras based on principles of geometry and optics. These models help in understanding and controlling how light from a 3D scene is projected onto a 2D image plane, which is essential for tasks like calibration, 3D reconstruction, and accurate image interpretation in machine vision. The primary geometrical image formation models include the pinhole camera model, perspective projection, and lens-based models.

## 1. Pinhole Camera Model

The pinhole camera model is a simplified representation of image formation, where light passes through a small hole (the "pinhole") and projects onto an image plane. This model is based on perspective projection, which ensures that light rays from the object converge at a single point on the image plane, preserving the relative positions and sizes of objects but without lens distortion.

### Characteristics of the Pinhole Camera Model

- **No Lens Distortion:** Assumes no lens, so no distortion effects are considered, making it a mathematically simple model.
- **Projection Geometry:** Light rays travel in straight lines from each point in the 3D scene through the pinhole and onto the image plane, forming an inverted image.
- **Image Formation Equation:** Given an object point $P(X,Y,Z)$ in 3D space, its image point $p(x,y)$ on the 2D image plane can be computed as: $x = f \cdot XZ$, $y = f \cdot YZ$ where $f$ is the focal length (distance from the pinhole to the image plane), and $Z$ is the depth of the object along the optical axis.

### Advantages and Limitations

- **Advantages:** The pinhole model is simple and effective for understanding the basic principles of image projection, and it forms the basis of more complex models.
- **Limitations:** It lacks realism due to the absence of a lens, meaning it does not account for blurring, distortion, or brightness variations, which are significant in real cameras.

## 2. Perspective Projection Model

The perspective projection model expands on the pinhole camera model by focusing on how points in 3D space map to points in 2D according to the rules of perspective. This model is useful for understanding image scaling and how objects appear smaller as they move farther from the camera.

### Characteristics of Perspective Projection

- **Principal Point:** The point on the image plane that lies on the optical axis is called the principal point, where light rays from the optical center intersect the image plane.
- **Vanishing Points:** Parallel lines in 3D space converge to a point (or points) in the 2D image, known as the vanishing points, due to perspective effects.
- **Projection Equations:** For an object point $P(X,Y,Z)$, the coordinates on the 2D image plane, $(u,v)(u,v)(u,v)$, can be derived with the perspective projection matrix as follows: $(u\ v\ 1) = (f\ 0\ u0,\ 0\ f\ v0,\ 0\ 0\ 1) \cdot \frac{1}{Z}(X\ Y\ Z)$ where $f$ is the focal length, and $(u0, v0)$ are the coordinates of the principal point on the image

plane.

## Applications

Perspective projection is essential for camera calibration, 3D reconstruction, and object measurement, as it relates 3D objects to their 2D images in a mathematically precise way.

## 3. Lens-Based Models

In real-world cameras, lenses are used to gather and focus light, affecting the way images are formed due to properties like refraction, focal length, and lens distortion.

### Thin Lens Model

The thin lens model is a simplified model for a lens system, where a single lens with focal length fff focuses light onto the image plane.

- **Thin Lens Equation:** The thin lens equation relates the object distance do, the image distance di, and the focal length f: $1/f = 1/do + 1/di$
- **Magnification:** The magnification of the image can be calculated as: $m = -di/do$ where a negative sign indicates an inverted image.

### Radial and Tangential Distortion

Real lenses introduce distortions that cause deviations from the ideal projection. The two main types are radial distortion and tangential distortion:

- **Radial Distortion:** Caused by the curvature of the lens, it makes straight lines appear curved, particularly toward the edges. Radial distortion is commonly seen in wide-angle lenses and is typically classified as barrel (curves outwards) or pincushion (curves inwards) distortion.
- **Tangential Distortion:** Caused by imperfections in lens alignment, leading to slight tilting or displacement of image points.
- **Correction Equations:** Distortion correction can be applied using polynomial models. For radial distortion, an approximation might be: $x' = x(1 + k1r^2 + k2r^4 + \dots)$ where k1,k2 are distortion coefficients, and r is the radial distance from the principal point.

### Applications of Lens-Based Models

Lens-based models are crucial for calibrating cameras to correct for distortion, ensuring accurate measurements, and enabling high-quality 3D reconstructions.

## 4. Homogeneous Coordinates and Transformation Matrices

In geometrical modeling, homogeneous coordinates and transformation matrices simplify the projection and transformation processes. This is especially important when working with multiple coordinate systems, such as world coordinates, camera coordinates, and image coordinates.

### Camera Transformation Matrix

The camera transformation matrix, often called the extrinsic matrix, describes the camera's position and orientation in relation to the world. It combines rotation and translation transformations: Extrinsic Matrix=(R T, 0 1) where R is the rotation matrix and T is the translation vector.

## Intrinsic Matrix

The intrinsic matrix describes the internal parameters of the camera, including focal length, principal point, and pixel scaling: Intrinsic Matrix=(fx 0 u0, 0 fy v0, 0 0 1) where fx and fy are the focal lengths in pixel units (taking into account pixel aspect ratio), and (u0,v0) is the principal point.

## Full Projection Model

Combining intrinsic and extrinsic parameters, the full 3D-to-2D projection of a point PPP in the world coordinates to the image point ppp in homogeneous coordinates can be represented as:

$$p=K[R \mid T]P$$

where K is the intrinsic matrix and $[R \mid T]$ is the extrinsic matrix.

## Applications of Geometrical Image Formation Models

- **Camera Calibration:** By applying geometrical models, camera parameters (intrinsic and extrinsic) can be estimated to improve accuracy, correct distortion, and enable precise measurements.
- **3D Reconstruction:** Geometrical models allow 3D scene reconstruction from 2D images by back-projecting points into space.
- **Object Measurement:** Enables accurate measurement of object dimensions in real-world units by understanding the mapping between 3D and 2D coordinates.
- **Pose Estimation:** Using models to determine the position and orientation of objects or cameras within a scene.

## Summary

Geometrical image formation models are foundational in machine vision, defining how 3D points are projected into 2D images:

- **Pinhole Camera Model:** A simplified perspective projection model without lens effects, useful for basic understanding.
- **Perspective Projection Model:** Adds realism, accounting for vanishing points and depth scaling.
- **Lens-Based Models:** Incorporate lens properties, such as focal length and distortion, to achieve more accurate and realistic projections.
- **Homogeneous Coordinates and Transformation Matrices:** Facilitate complex transformations across multiple coordinate systems, essential for calibration, measurement, and 3D reconstruction.

These models play a crucial role in applications requiring precise control and understanding of image formation, such as calibration, measurement, and 3D imaging.

# Camera Calibration

Camera calibration is the process of determining a camera's internal parameters (intrinsic parameters) and its position and orientation in space (extrinsic parameters) to accurately map 3D points in the real world to 2D points on an image plane. Calibration is essential in machine vision, robotics, and 3D reconstruction applications to achieve accurate measurements, correct distortion, and ensure precise image analysis.

## Why Camera Calibration is Important

1. **Distortion Correction:** Real-world cameras, especially those with lenses, introduce distortions (e.g., radial and tangential distortion). Calibration helps correct these distortions so that images accurately represent the scene.
2. **Accurate Measurement and 3D Reconstruction:** For applications requiring precise measurements or 3D reconstruction (e.g., in quality control, robotic navigation), calibration ensures that the spatial relationships between objects are accurately represented in the image.
3. **Pose Estimation:** In applications like augmented reality or robotics, knowing the camera's position and orientation relative to the objects in the scene allows for accurate overlay and interaction with real-world elements.

## Key Components of Camera Calibration

Camera calibration involves determining two main sets of parameters:

**Intrinsic Parameters:** These parameters define the internal characteristics of the camera, such as focal length, principal point, and distortion coefficients.

- **Focal Length (f):** The distance from the camera's optical center (or lens) to the image sensor. Often represented by $fx\_xfx$ and $fyf\_yfy$ in pixel units, which may differ due to sensor pixel aspect ratio.
- **Principal Point (u_0, v_0):** The point on the image sensor where the optical axis intersects the image plane. Ideally, this is at the center of the image, but real-world lenses can cause a slight offset.
- **Skew Coefficient:** Represents the angle between the sensor's x- and y-axis. In most cases, this is close to zero, but it can be included in calculations if the camera's sensor is not perfectly aligned.
- **Distortion Coefficients:** These coefficients model the lens distortion, including:
- **Radial Distortion:** Curves straight lines near the edges of the image, either bending outwards (barrel distortion) or inwards (pincushion distortion).
- **Tangential Distortion:** Occurs if the lens is not perfectly aligned with the image plane, causing the image to tilt slightly.

**Extrinsic Parameters:** These define the camera's position and orientation relative to the scene or world coordinates.

- **Rotation Matrix (R):** Defines the camera's orientation in space by describing the rotation needed to align the camera's coordinate system with the world's coordinate system.
- **Translation Vector (T):** Defines the camera's position in the world coordinate system by describing the translation needed to move the camera's origin to the world origin.

## Calibration Process Overview

The camera calibration process typically involves capturing images of a known pattern (e.g., a checkerboard) from multiple angles and then using software to estimate the intrinsic and extrinsic parameters based on these images. Here's a step-by-step outline:

1. **Image Acquisition:** Capture multiple images of a calibration pattern (usually a checkerboard or a dot grid) from various angles and distances. The pattern provides a set of points with known coordinates in the world frame.
2. **Feature Detection:** Detect key points in the calibration pattern (e.g., the corners of the checkerboard squares). These points have known coordinates in the real world, making them easy to map in the calibration process.
3. **Parameter Estimation:** Use algorithms (like the Zhang's calibration method) to estimate the intrinsic and extrinsic parameters. The algorithm calculates how the known 3D points on the pattern project onto the 2D image plane and adjusts parameters to minimize the error between the observed and expected projections.
4. **Distortion Correction:** Compute distortion coefficients and use them to create a correction map. This map allows images to be "undistorted" so that straight lines in the real world appear straight in the corrected image.
5. **Reprojection Error Calculation:** To assess calibration accuracy, compute the reprojection error—the difference between the observed 2D points and the projected 3D points. Lower reprojection error indicates a more accurate calibration.

## Calibration Models and Equations

**Intrinsic Matrix (K):** The intrinsic matrix encodes the intrinsic parameters, including focal length, principal point, and skew. It is represented as:

$$K=(fx\ s\ u0,\ 0\ fy\ v0,\ 0\ 0\ 1)$$

where $fx$ and $fy$ are the focal lengths in pixel units, $sss$ is the skew coefficient, and $(u0,v0)$ is the principal point.

**Extrinsic Matrix:** The extrinsic parameters are represented by a rotation matrix R and a translation vector T:

$$\text{Extrinsic Matrix}=(R\ T,\ 0\ 1)$$

where R and T describe the camera's position and orientation relative to the world coordinates.

**Projection Equation:** Combining intrinsic and extrinsic parameters, the projection of a 3D point $PPP$ (in world coordinates) onto the 2D image plane can be described as:

$$p = K(R\ T)P$$

where K is the intrinsic matrix, $(R \mid T)$ is the extrinsic matrix, and $ppp$ is the projected 2D point in homogeneous coordinates.

## Calibration Techniques

- **Checkerboard Calibration:** The most common technique, where images of a checkerboard pattern are used. The known geometry of the checkerboard (square size and spacing) allows for precise feature detection and parameter estimation.
- **Dot Grid Calibration:** Similar to checkerboard calibration but uses a grid of dots, which can be useful in situations where a checkerboard pattern is hard to use.
- **Self-Calibration:** Techniques that use natural features in the environment rather than a calibration pattern. This is more complex and less accurate than using known patterns but can be useful for mobile systems where standard calibration may be impractical.

## Calibration Software and Tools

Several software tools are commonly used for camera calibration:

- **OpenCV:** An open-source computer vision library that includes robust calibration functions. It supports checkerboard and dot grid calibration.
- **MATLAB Camera Calibration Toolbox:** A popular tool in academia and industry for calibrating single and stereo cameras, offering advanced calibration and visualization options.
- **ROS (Robot Operating System):** Provides tools for camera calibration specifically aimed at robotics applications, allowing easy integration into robotic vision systems.

## Applications of Camera Calibration

- **3D Reconstruction:** Calibrated cameras allow for accurate 3D modeling and reconstruction from multiple views, essential for industrial inspections and mapping applications.
- **Augmented Reality (AR):** Calibration ensures virtual objects align accurately with the real world, enhancing AR experience.
- **Robotic Vision:** Robots rely on calibrated cameras for tasks like object recognition, localization, and navigation in structured and unstructured environments.
- **Measurement and Inspection:** Calibration allows for precise measurement of objects in real-world units, making it essential in quality control and industrial inspection systems.

## Summary

Camera calibration is a fundamental process in machine vision and 3D imaging, ensuring that images accurately represent real-world scenes by correcting lens distortions and mapping 3D coordinates to the 2D image plane. The process involves:

- **Intrinsic Calibration:** Determining internal camera properties like focal length, principal point, and distortion coefficients.
- **Extrinsic Calibration:** Determining the camera's position and orientation relative to the scene.
- **Distortion Correction:** Correcting lens distortions to ensure straight lines in the world appear straight in images.
- **Projection Modeling:** Applying the camera model to accurately map 3D world points to 2D image points.

By calibrating a camera, we can ensure that it produces accurate, distortion-free images suitable for tasks that require high precision, such as robotic navigation, 3D reconstruction, and industrial inspection.

# 2 Mark Questions

1. What are scene constraints in machine vision?
2. Define lighting parameters in the context of machine vision.
3. Name two common lighting sources used in machine vision systems.
4. What factors are considered in selecting a lighting source for machine vision?
5. Explain the importance of lighting techniques in machine vision.
6. Differentiate between front lighting and backlighting techniques.
7. List two types of lenses used in machine vision.
8. Why are optical filters important in machine vision applications?
9. What is the main difference between CCD and CMOS imaging sensors?
10. List two specifications to consider when selecting a CCD or CMOS sensor.
11. Describe one advantage of using a CMOS sensor over a CCD sensor.
12. What is meant by interface architecture in the context of imaging sensors?
13. Compare analog and digital cameras in terms of signal transmission.
14. Mention two types of digital camera interfaces commonly used in machine vision.
15. What is the role of camera-computer interfaces in a machine vision system?
16. Name two key specifications to consider when selecting a camera-computer interface.
17. What is the purpose of geometrical image formation models in machine vision?
18. Define the pinhole camera model in simple terms.
19. What is the purpose of camera calibration in machine vision?
20. How does camera calibration help in correcting lens distortion?

# 15 Mark Questions

1. Explain the concept of scene constraints in machine vision systems. Discuss how these constraints affect image acquisition and provide examples of strategies to manage or overcome these challenges in industrial applications.
2. Discuss the role of lighting parameters in machine vision. How do parameters like intensity, angle, color, and uniformity impact the quality of captured images? Illustrate with examples of how different lighting parameters are adjusted to suit specific applications.
3. Describe the selection criteria for lighting sources in machine vision. Compare the advantages and disadvantages of various lighting sources, such as LEDs, fluorescent, and fiber-optic lighting, and provide examples of applications where each is most appropriate.
4. Explain the different lighting techniques used in machine vision, including backlighting, front lighting, side lighting, and ring lighting. Discuss the advantages and applications of each technique, highlighting situations where each technique would be optimal.
5. Discuss the importance of lenses and optical filters in machine vision systems. How do lens specifications like focal length, aperture, and distortion influence image quality? Describe the process of selecting an appropriate lens and optical filter for an application.
6. Compare CCD and CMOS imaging sensors. Discuss their working principles, specifications, advantages, and disadvantages, and describe scenarios where each type of sensor would be the preferred choice in machine vision applications.
7. Explain the different interface architectures for imaging sensors in machine vision, including sequential (CCD) and parallel (CMOS) readout methods. How do these architectures impact factors such as speed, noise, and power consumption?
8. Discuss the differences between analog and digital cameras in machine vision. Explain how signal transmission, resolution, and integration with modern systems differ between the two, and provide examples of applications suited to each type of camera.
9. Describe the types of digital camera interfaces used in machine vision systems, such as USB, GigE, Camera Link, and CoaXPress. Discuss the specifications, advantages, and ideal applications for each interface, focusing on data rate, cable length, and power delivery capabilities.
10. Explain the key considerations in selecting a camera-computer interface for a machine vision application. Discuss specifications like data rate, latency, power delivery, and compatibility, and explain how each factor influences interface selection for different industrial scenarios.
11. Describe geometrical image formation models, focusing on the pinhole camera model and perspective projection. Explain how these models are used to map 3D points in the real world to 2D points on an image plane and discuss their relevance in camera calibration and 3D reconstruction.
12. What is camera calibration in machine vision, and why is it essential? Describe the steps involved in calibrating a camera, including intrinsic and extrinsic parameter estimation, and explain how calibration helps in distortion correction and accurate 3D measurements.

# IMAGE PROCESSING

Machine Vision Software – Fundamentals of Digital Image – Image Acquisition Modes – Image Processing in Spatial and Frequency Domain – Point Operation, Thresholding, Grayscale Stretching – Neighborhood Operations, Image Smoothing and Sharpening – Edge Detection – Binary Morphology – Colour image processing.

# Machine Vision Software

Machine Vision Software is designed to enable computers or machines to interpret and process visual data, like images or videos, in a way that mimics human vision. It's commonly used in industries like manufacturing, robotics, healthcare, and security, where machines need to analyze visual information for quality control, automation, and inspection tasks. Here's an overview of how it works and some key components:

### 1. How It Works

- **Image Acquisition:** The software first captures an image or video from cameras or other imaging sensors.
- **Preprocessing:** It enhances image quality to make subsequent processing steps more accurate. This can involve filtering, noise reduction, or adjusting contrast and brightness.
- **Feature Extraction:** Key features such as edges, textures, colors, or patterns are identified. These features are crucial for recognizing specific objects or characteristics in the image.
- **Pattern Recognition and Analysis:** The software applies algorithms, often powered by artificial intelligence (AI) and machine learning (ML), to recognize objects, classify parts, or identify defects. This step is central to quality inspection and defect detection.
- **Decision Making and Output:** Based on the analysis, the system makes a decision or triggers an action, such as sorting items, rejecting defective products, or guiding robots for assembly tasks.

### 2. Key Components of Machine Vision Software

- **Imaging Libraries:** Provide functions for image processing, computer vision tasks, and sometimes pre-trained models for object recognition. Examples include OpenCV, HALCON, and MATLAB's Image Processing Toolbox.
- **Machine Learning Models:** Deep learning models (e.g., convolutional neural networks) are frequently used to improve accuracy in complex recognition tasks, like identifying different product types or detecting subtle defects.
- **User Interface and Customization Tools:** Many machine vision software solutions have intuitive UIs that allow engineers to adjust settings, define regions of interest, and customize detection criteria.
- **Communication Protocols:** Most machine vision systems integrate with industrial networks or machine controllers (PLC, SCADA) to communicate inspection results or control commands.

### 3. Applications of Machine Vision Software

- **Quality Control and Inspection:** Detecting defects in products, like scratches, misalignments, or missing components.
- **Robotics and Automation:** Guiding robots in tasks such as pick-and-place, assembly, and bin picking.
- **Optical Character Recognition (OCR):** Recognizing printed text or labels, useful for sorting packages or checking serial numbers.
- **Object and Pattern Recognition:** Identifying specific objects or features for sorting or categorization.
- **Measurement and Gauging:** Measuring physical dimensions or distances in products for accuracy.

### 4. Popular Machine Vision Software Platforms

- **OpenCV:** Open-source library widely used for basic and advanced computer vision applications.
- **HALCON:** Offers a wide range of image processing and machine learning functions tailored for industrial use.
- **Matrox Imaging:** Provides vision software that integrates with hardware solutions for optimized performance in industrial settings.
- **NI Vision Development Module:** Part of National Instruments, offering tools specifically designed for quality inspection and automation.

In recent years, machine vision software has increasingly incorporated AI and deep learning, making it more adaptable to diverse applications and improving its accuracy in real-time.

# Fundamentals of Digital Image

The fundamentals of digital images lie in the concepts of capturing, representing, processing, and analyzing visual data in a digital format. Here's a breakdown of the essential concepts:

## 1. What is a Digital Image?

- A digital image is a representation of a two-dimensional (2D) visual scene as a grid of pixels (picture elements), each of which has a specific color or intensity value.
- Digital images can be captured by cameras, scanners, or other sensors and are stored as a matrix of numbers (pixels), where each number represents the intensity of light at that point.

## 2. Pixels and Resolution

- **Pixels:** The smallest unit of a digital image, representing a single point in the image. Each pixel contains information about color or brightness.
- **Resolution:** The total number of pixels in an image, often described by its width and height (e.g., 1920x1080 pixels). Higher resolution provides more detail, but it also increases file size.

## 3. Color Representation

- Digital images can be grayscale or color. Grayscale images represent different intensities of gray, from black to white, while color images represent a wide spectrum of colors.
  - **Color Models:** Common color models include:
- **RGB (Red, Green, Blue):** Each pixel is represented by three values (one for each primary color). Combining different intensities of these colors produces the full color spectrum.
  - **CMYK (Cyan, Magenta, Yellow, Black):** Used mainly in printing.
- **HSV (Hue, Saturation, Value):** A model that separates color information (hue) from intensity (value) and purity (saturation).

## 4. Image Depth or Bit Depth

- Bit depth refers to the number of bits used to represent each pixel's color information.
- **8-bit images:** Each color channel (RGB) has 256 possible values (0 to 255), allowing for around 16.7 million colors in total (8 bits per channel).
- Higher bit depths (e.g., 16-bit or 32-bit) increase the number of colors but also require more storage and processing power.

## 5. Spatial and Frequency Domains

- **Spatial Domain:** Represents image information as it is, in terms of pixel locations and intensities.
- **Frequency Domain:** Describes an image based on its frequency components, which can reveal patterns, edges, or textures more clearly. Techniques like the Fourier Transform are used to convert images between spatial and frequency domains for various processing tasks (e.g., sharpening, blurring).

## 6. Image Processing Techniques

- **Filtering:** Applying filters to enhance or suppress certain features, like blurring to reduce noise or edge detection to highlight boundaries.
- **Histogram Equalization:** A technique to adjust contrast by spreading out the most frequent intensity values, enhancing visibility in under- or overexposed areas.
- **Transformations:** Applying transformations (e.g., scaling, rotation, or affine transformations) changes the geometry of the image, used in image alignment or correction.
- **Morphological Operations:** Used mainly for binary images, morphological operations (like erosion and dilation) can help with object detection by refining shapes or eliminating noise.

## 7. Image Compression

- Digital images often require compression to reduce file size. Compression can be lossless (preserving all original data) or lossy (reducing data for smaller sizes but losing some details).
  - JPEG is a common lossy format for photographs, balancing quality and size.
  - PNG is a popular lossless format for web graphics, preserving detail without sacrificing quality.

## 8. Applications of Digital Images

- **Medical Imaging:** Used in radiology, MRI, and CT scans to diagnose diseases.
- **Remote Sensing:** Satellite and aerial imaging for environmental monitoring, agriculture, and urban planning.
- **Security and Surveillance:** For facial recognition, object tracking, and threat detection.
- **Augmented Reality (AR):** Superimposing digital images over real-world views in devices like smartphones and AR glasses.

## 9. Image Analysis and Computer Vision

- Digital images are also used in computer vision for object detection, classification, and tracking. Machine learning, especially deep learning, plays a significant role in analyzing digital images for automated recognition and decision-making.

Understanding these fundamentals helps in processing, enhancing, and interpreting digital images, enabling their use across a wide array of applications, from everyday photography to complex industrial and scientific tasks.

# Image Acquisition Modes

Image acquisition modes refer to the various methods or techniques used to capture images, each designed for specific conditions, requirements, and imaging devices. In fields like industrial automation, medical imaging, and remote sensing, choosing the right acquisition mode is critical for getting accurate and relevant visual data. Here's an overview of some common image acquisition modes:

### 1. Single Image Acquisition

- **Definition:** This mode captures a single, static image at a specific time.
- **Applications:** Often used in applications where a single snapshot is sufficient, like photographing stationary objects or taking still medical images (e.g., X-rays).
- **Advantages:** Simple, quick, and requires minimal processing power.
- **Limitations:** Not suitable for capturing motion or dynamic changes.

### 2. Continuous or Video Acquisition

- **Definition:** In continuous or video mode, images are captured in a rapid, sequential flow, often at high frame rates, producing video or continuous image streams.
- **Applications:** Commonly used in security surveillance, real-time tracking, and robotics where continuous monitoring is needed.
- **Advantages:** Allows real-time monitoring and is ideal for observing changes over time.
- **Limitations:** Requires more storage and processing power due to high data rates.

### 3. Triggered or Event-Based Acquisition

- **Definition:** Images are captured only when a specific event or trigger occurs, such as a signal from a sensor or a command from an external system.
- **Applications:** Used in quality control, industrial inspection, and automated assembly lines where images are needed only when a part reaches a specific location or an event takes place.
- **Advantages:** Saves storage and processing power by capturing only relevant moments.
- **Limitations:** Requires precise triggering mechanisms and can miss events if not configured correctly.

### 4. Time-Lapse Acquisition

- **Definition:** Images are captured at set intervals over time, creating a sequence that shows gradual changes in the scene.
- **Applications:** Ideal for capturing processes that unfold over hours or days, like plant growth, construction projects, or long-term scientific experiments.
- **Advantages:** Enables observation of slow processes by compressing time in the resulting sequence.
- **Limitations:** Can miss rapid changes, and the intervals must be carefully chosen to capture all necessary data.

### 5. Burst Mode Acquisition

- **Definition:** A series of images is captured in rapid succession with minimal delay between each frame, effectively freezing motion in high-speed scenes.
- **Applications:** Commonly used in sports photography, wildlife monitoring, and any fast-moving scene where detail is essential.
- **Advantages:** Captures fast action in detail, allowing for post-capture selection of the best frames.
- **Limitations:** Consumes significant storage and processing power and may require a fast shutter and high-speed sensors.

## 6. Multi-Spectral and Hyper-Spectral Acquisition

- **Definition:** Captures images in multiple spectral bands, often beyond the visible spectrum, such as infrared, ultraviolet, or other specific wavelengths.
- **Applications:** Widely used in remote sensing, agriculture, environmental monitoring, and medical imaging to identify materials, vegetation health, and other details not visible in standard imaging.
- **Advantages:** Provides detailed information about materials and conditions that aren't apparent in visible light.
- **Limitations:** Requires specialized sensors and can result in large data sizes that need complex processing.

## 7. Stereo or 3D Imaging Acquisition

- **Definition:** Captures images from two or more slightly different angles, creating depth information and allowing for 3D reconstruction.
- **Applications:** Used in 3D scanning, autonomous vehicles, augmented reality, and robotics for depth perception and spatial awareness.
- **Advantages:** Provides 3D spatial information and can be used for accurate distance measurements.
- **Limitations:** Requires precise alignment and calibration of multiple cameras, increasing hardware and computational complexity.

## 8. Line-Scan or Line-by-Line Acquisition

- **Definition:** Captures images line by line, where each line represents a single row of pixels, typically used in conveyor belt systems or applications where the scene moves continuously in one direction.
- **Applications:** Used in industrial inspection, where objects move past the camera (e.g., quality inspection on assembly lines).
- **Advantages:** Ideal for scanning large objects or continuously moving surfaces.
- **Limitations:** Limited to applications with a steady, uniform motion, as sudden changes can cause distortion in the image.

## 9. Region of Interest (ROI) Acquisition

- **Definition:** Only a specific area or "region of interest" within the full sensor view is captured or processed.
- **Applications:** Often used in applications that need to focus on a small part of the scene, like monitoring a particular machine part or a face in surveillance.
- **Advantages:** Reduces data processing load by focusing only on necessary areas.
- **Limitations:** If the ROI is not correctly defined, important data outside the region may be missed.

Each acquisition mode is suited to particular types of imaging tasks, depending on factors like the object's speed, environmental conditions, and the need for depth or spectral data.

# Image Processing in Spatial and Frequency Domain

Image processing in both the spatial and frequency domains involves manipulating images to enhance, analyze, or extract information. While spatial domain processing works directly with pixel values, frequency domain processing transforms the image into a representation based on frequencies, allowing for different types of enhancements and manipulations.

## 1. Spatial Domain Processing

In the spatial domain, image processing involves direct manipulation of pixel values.

- **Techniques:** Common spatial domain techniques include filtering, contrast enhancement, histogram equalization, and image restoration.
- **Mathematical Representation:** Spatial domain processing can be represented as a function $f(x,y)$ applied directly to the pixel values, where $x$ and $y$ are pixel coordinates.

### Key Spatial Domain Techniques

- **Point Operations:** Operate on individual pixel values. Examples include brightness adjustments (adding a constant to pixel values) and contrast adjustments (scaling pixel values).
- **Neighborhood Operations:** Use a small region (neighborhood) around each pixel to calculate a new pixel value, typically using a kernel or filter. Examples include:
  - **Smoothing (Blurring):** Reduces noise or detail by averaging pixel values in a local area, commonly achieved using low-pass filters like a Gaussian filter.
  - **Sharpening:** Enhances edges and fine details using high-pass filters, such as the Laplacian or Sobel operators, which highlight changes in intensity.
  - **Histogram-Based Processing:** Techniques like histogram equalization improve image contrast by redistributing pixel intensities across the available range.
- **Morphological Operations:** Applied mainly to binary images to refine shapes, remove noise, or perform tasks like edge detection. Examples include dilation, erosion, opening, and closing.

### Advantages of Spatial Domain Processing

- Simple and computationally efficient for basic tasks.
- Suitable for enhancing specific areas in images, especially with localized modifications.
  - Limitations of Spatial Domain Processing
- Limited effectiveness for frequency-based adjustments (e.g., separating noise and signal components).
- Some image features, like periodic patterns, are better analyzed in the frequency domain.

## 2. Frequency Domain Processing

In the frequency domain, image processing manipulates the frequency components of an image, which is often transformed using the Fourier Transform.

- **Transformation:** The Fourier Transform converts an image from the spatial domain (pixel values) to the frequency domain, representing it in terms of its sinusoidal frequency components. In this domain, each point represents a specific frequency within the image, with low frequencies representing smooth areas and high frequencies corresponding to edges or sharp details.

- **Mathematical Representation:** The Discrete Fourier Transform (DFT) is commonly used to represent an image in the frequency domain, transforming the image function $f(x,y)$ into $F(u,v)$, where $u$ and $v$ represent frequency components.

## Key Frequency Domain Techniques

- **Filtering in Frequency Domain:** Filters are applied to emphasize or suppress specific frequencies in the image. Common techniques include:
  - **Low-Pass Filtering:** Attenuates high-frequency components (edges and noise) while preserving low-frequency components (smooth regions). This results in blurring or noise reduction.
  - **High-Pass Filtering:** Enhances high-frequency components, emphasizing edges and fine details.
  - **Band-Pass Filtering:** Allows a specific range of frequencies to pass through while blocking others, useful in applications like texture analysis.
- **Fourier Transform Applications:** Specific patterns, such as repetitive textures or noise, can be analyzed in the frequency domain. By manipulating the frequency representation, selective enhancements or reductions are possible, which is particularly useful for applications like image compression and noise filtering.
- **Inverse Fourier Transform:** After applying filters or other manipulations in the frequency domain, the Inverse Fourier Transform converts the image back to the spatial domain.

## Advantages of Frequency Domain Processing

- **Selective Filtering:** Allows specific frequency components (e.g., noise or texture) to be targeted, which can be more challenging in the spatial domain.
- **Image Compression:** Frequency domain transformations, like the Discrete Cosine Transform (DCT) used in JPEG compression, make it easier to compress images by discarding less important frequency components.
- **Pattern Recognition:** Identifies periodic patterns and textures more effectively, which is helpful in applications like defect detection and fingerprint analysis.

## Limitations of Frequency Domain Processing

- Computationally more intensive than spatial domain processing, especially for large images.
- Less intuitive, as working with frequency components rather than pixel values requires specific expertise and understanding.

In practice, both domains are often used together. For instance, spatial techniques are suitable for initial noise reduction or sharpening, while frequency domain methods handle complex filtering or compression tasks.

# Point Operation, Thresholding, Grayscale Stretching

Point operations, thresholding, and grayscale stretching are fundamental image processing techniques used to manipulate the pixel intensity values in an image, mainly for contrast adjustment, enhancement, and object detection. Here's an explanation of each:

### 1. Point Operations

- **Definition:** Point operations are transformations applied independently to each pixel in an image without considering neighboring pixels. The output intensity of each pixel is determined by a function applied to its original intensity.
- **Formula:** If $f(x,y)$ is the original pixel intensity and $g(x,y)$ is the transformed pixel intensity, then the transformation can be represented as: $g(x,y)=T(f(x,y))$ where $T$ is a predefined function applied to each pixel.
- **Applications:** Point operations are used for brightness and contrast adjustments, color transformations, and basic image enhancements.

### Common Types of Point Operations:

- **Brightness Adjustment:** Adding a constant value to each pixel to increase or decrease the brightness.
- **Contrast Adjustment:** Multiplying each pixel value by a factor to change the range of pixel intensities, enhancing image contrast.
- **Negative Transformation:** Inverts the image by subtracting each pixel value from the maximum intensity, making bright areas dark and vice versa.

### 2. Thresholding

- **Definition:** Thresholding is a simple, effective point operation technique that converts an image into a binary image (black and white) based on a threshold value. Pixels above the threshold are set to one value (often white), and pixels below it are set to another (often black).

### Types of Thresholding:

- **Global Thresholding:** A single threshold value is applied to the entire image.
- **Adaptive Thresholding:** The threshold value varies across different regions in the image, useful for images with varying lighting conditions.
- **Otsu's Method:** An automatic thresholding technique that determines the optimal threshold by minimizing intra-class variance (the variance within the foreground and background).
- **Applications:** Thresholding is widely used in segmentation, especially in detecting objects from backgrounds in applications like medical imaging, document scanning, and industrial inspection.

### 3. Grayscale Stretching (Contrast Stretching)

- **Definition:** Grayscale stretching, or contrast stretching, enhances image contrast by expanding the range of grayscale values across the available range, often from 0 to 255 in 8-bit images. This process redistributes pixel intensity values to cover the full grayscale spectrum, improving visibility of details in under- or over-exposed images.

- **Formula:** For an original image with minimum and maximum intensity values fmin and fmax, grayscale stretching can be represented as: $g(x,y)=(f(x,y)-fmin)\times(gmax-gmin)/(fmax-fmin)+gmin$ where gmin and gmax are the new minimum and maximum intensities (often 0 and 255).
- **Applications:** Grayscale stretching is used to enhance low-contrast images, like medical images, satellite photos, and poorly illuminated photographs.

These operations are simple but powerful tools for enhancing and analyzing images, serving as foundational steps in many image processing workflows.

# Neighborhood Operations, Image Smoothing and Sharpening

Neighborhood operations, image smoothing, and sharpening are crucial techniques in image processing used to modify pixel values based on the values of neighboring pixels. These techniques are particularly useful for enhancing image features, reducing noise, and improving visual quality. Here's an overview:

## 1. Neighborhood Operations

- **Definition:** Neighborhood operations involve processing each pixel based on the values of surrounding pixels, typically within a small matrix called a kernel or filter. The kernel moves across the image, applying specific transformations to the local region of each pixel.
- **Kernel Size:** The kernel's size is often 3x3, 5x5, or larger depending on the task, with the center pixel being the target pixel for processing. The kernel size and type determine the effect on the image.

### Key Uses of Neighborhood Operations:

- **Image Smoothing:** Reduces noise by averaging or blurring the pixels within the neighborhood.
- **Image Sharpening:** Enhances edges by emphasizing differences between the pixel and its neighbors.
- **Edge Detection:** Highlights edges by identifying areas of high intensity change within neighborhoods.
- Neighborhood operations can be further categorized based on the type of kernel used and the intended outcome, as seen in image smoothing and sharpening.

## 2. Image Smoothing (Blurring)

- **Purpose:** Smoothing (or blurring) is used to reduce noise and soften textures in an image. It is particularly useful in reducing detail that may not be necessary, such as small objects or grainy noise.
- **How It Works:** Smoothing kernels apply a weighted or unweighted average of the surrounding pixels to the central pixel, producing a softened effect.

### Types of Smoothing Techniques:

- **Average (Mean) Filtering:** Replaces each pixel with the average value of its neighborhood. This simple method reduces noise but can blur edges. $g(x,y)=1n^2\sum neighborhood f(x,y)$
- **Gaussian Filtering:** Applies a Gaussian-shaped kernel, which assigns higher weights to pixels closer to the center, resulting in a smoother, more natural blur that preserves some details.
- Gaussian filtering is widely used because it reduces high-frequency noise while maintaining overall structure better than simple averaging.
- **Median Filtering:** Replaces each pixel with the median value within its neighborhood. This is effective for reducing "salt-and-pepper" noise (random black and white spots) without excessively blurring edges.

### Applications of Smoothing:

- **Noise Reduction:** Removes unwanted artifacts (e.g., sensor noise in photos).
- **Preprocessing:** Prepares images for edge detection or segmentation by reducing minor details that could interfere with feature extraction.

<h3 align="center">3. Image Sharpening</h3>

- **Purpose:** Sharpening enhances edges and fine details, making the image appear crisper and more defined. It is particularly useful for highlighting boundaries between objects or making details more visible.
  - **How It Works:** Sharpening emphasizes the differences between a pixel and its neighbors, often using kernels that highlight high-frequency components in the image.

<h3 align="center">Types of Sharpening Techniques:</h3>

- **Laplacian Filtering:** Uses a kernel based on the Laplacian operator, which calculates the second derivative of the image. This operator highlights areas of rapid intensity change (edges).

$$g(x,y)=f(x,y)-\text{Laplacian}(f(x,y))$$

- **Unsharp Masking:** A common technique that subtracts a blurred version of the image from the original to enhance edges.

1. First, the image is smoothed (blurred).
2. The blurred image is then subtracted from the original, emphasizing the edges.
3. The difference is added back to the original image to create the sharpened effect.

- **High-Pass Filtering:** Allows high-frequency (sharp detail) components to pass while attenuating low-frequency (smooth areas) components. High-pass filters remove gradual intensity changes, keeping edges and details.

<h3 align="center">Applications of Sharpening:</h3>

- **Enhancing Detail:** Used in photography and medical imaging to make images crisper and highlight small structures.
- **Edge Enhancement:** Important for object recognition, making boundaries clearer and easier to detect in subsequent processing stages.

These techniques play complementary roles in image processing: smoothing removes unwanted noise and artifacts, while sharpening enhances edges and fine details, allowing for more detailed analysis or improved visual quality.

# Edge detection

Edge detection is a fundamental technique in image processing that identifies points in an image where there is a significant change in intensity, indicating boundaries between different regions, objects, or features. These changes often represent edges, which are crucial for understanding the structure, shape, and contours in an image. Edge detection is essential for tasks such as object recognition, image segmentation, and pattern recognition.

## Key Concepts in Edge Detection

- **Edge:** An edge is a line or boundary that separates regions of different intensities in an image.
- **Gradient:** The gradient measures the change in intensity values in an image, with high gradients indicating potential edges.
- **Edge Direction:** The direction of the gradient (change) indicates the orientation of the edge.

## Steps in Edge Detection

1. **Noise Reduction:** Since noise can produce false edges, a smoothing filter (such as Gaussian) is often applied before edge detection.
2. **Gradient Calculation:** The gradient of the image is computed to measure the rate of intensity change at each pixel.
3. **Thresholding:** The gradient magnitudes are thresholded to keep only significant edges, removing low gradients that are likely due to noise or minor intensity variations.
4. **Edge Linking and Localization:** Some algorithms connect edge points to form continuous edges, improving the consistency and clarity of detected boundaries.

## Common Edge Detection Techniques

### 1. Sobel Operator

- **Description:** The Sobel operator uses two 3x3 kernels (filters) to calculate approximate gradients in the horizontal and vertical directions. The gradient magnitude gives the edge strength, while the direction is used to determine the orientation.
- **Formula:** Given an image f(x,y), the Sobel gradient magnitudes Gx and Gy are calculated as: $G = \sqrt{G\_x^2 + G\_y^2}$
- **Applications:** Sobel is commonly used for edge detection in basic applications where noise is minimal. It's fast but sensitive to noise.

### 2. Prewitt Operator

- **Description:** Similar to the Sobel operator, the Prewitt operator also calculates the gradient in the x and y directions but uses slightly different kernel values.
- **Formula:** Like Sobel, it computes: $G = \sqrt{G\_x^2 + G\_y^2}$
- **Applications:** The Prewitt operator is simpler but less accurate in gradient approximation than Sobel, suitable for images with minimal noise.

### 3. Laplacian of Gaussian (LoG)

- **Description:** The Laplacian of Gaussian combines Gaussian smoothing and Laplacian edge detection in one step. First, a Gaussian filter is used to smooth the image, reducing noise, followed by applying the Laplacian operator to find areas of rapid intensity change.
  - **Formula:** The Laplacian of an image f(x,y) is given by: $\nabla^2 f = \partial^2 f / \partial x^2 + \partial^2 f / \partial y^2$
- **Applications:** The LoG is more effective at detecting edges in noisy images since it reduces noise beforehand, commonly used in scientific and industrial applications.

### 4. Canny Edge Detector

- **Description:** The Canny edge detector is a multi-step, advanced method known for its ability to detect sharp edges while minimizing noise.

### Steps:

1. **Gaussian Smoothing:** Reduces noise.
2. **Gradient Calculation:** Computes the intensity gradient.
3. **Non-Maximum Suppression:** Thin out the edges by keeping only the local maximum gradient points.
4. **Double Thresholding:** Applies two thresholds (high and low) to classify strong and weak edges.
5. **Edge Tracking by Hysteresis:** Connects weak edges to strong edges, forming continuous lines.

**Applications:** The Canny edge detector is widely used in computer vision and medical imaging for its balance of precision and noise reduction.

### 5. Roberts Cross Operator

- **Description:** The Roberts Cross operator is an older, simpler method that uses two 2x2 kernels to approximate the gradient at a pixel.
  - **Formula:** Computes the gradient by applying the following kernels: $Gx = f(x,y) - f(x+1,y+1)$, $Gy = f(x+1,y) - f(x,y+1)$
- **Applications:** Suitable for images with sharp edges and minimal noise. Its small kernel size makes it fast but more sensitive to noise than larger operators.

### Applications of Edge Detection

- **Object Detection and Recognition:** Identifying objects or features by their edges, such as in facial recognition, vehicle detection, or item identification.
- **Image Segmentation:** Separating an image into distinct regions or objects based on detected edges.
- **Medical Imaging:** Detecting anatomical boundaries (e.g., organs or tumors) for analysis and diagnosis.
- **Robotics and Computer Vision:** Used in path planning, object tracking, and scene understanding for autonomous vehicles and robots.

Edge detection is a foundational step in many image processing workflows, enhancing the ability to detect structures and forms within images. Selecting the appropriate method depends on factors such as noise level, computational resources, and the specific requirements of the task at hand.

# Binary Morphology

Binary morphology in image processing is a set of operations that processes binary images (images with only two pixel values, typically black and white) to analyze and manipulate the shapes and structures within the image. Morphological operations focus on the structure or "shape" of objects within an image and are particularly useful for tasks like object detection, image segmentation, and noise removal.

## Basics of Binary Morphology

- **Binary Image:** A binary image contains only two pixel values, often 0 (black) for the background and 1 (white) for the objects.
- **Structuring Element:** Morphological operations use a small, predefined shape called a structuring element (SE), which acts as a probe to examine the shape and structure of the objects. The SE can take various shapes, such as a square, circle, cross, or rectangle, and its size and shape determine the operation's effect.
- **Set Theory:** Morphological operations are based on set theory and involve adding or removing pixels from the objects based on the spatial relationship with their neighbors.

## Key Binary Morphological Operations

### 1. Erosion

- **Definition:** Erosion removes pixels from the edges of objects in the binary image, effectively shrinking or "eroding" the objects. It only keeps pixels at locations where the structuring element fully fits within the object.
- **How It Works:** The structuring element moves across the image, and a pixel in the output image is set to 1 only if all pixels under the structuring element in the input image are also 1.
- **Effects:** Reduces the size of objects, removes small noise or isolated pixels, and can separate close objects.
- **Applications:** Erosion is useful for removing small artifacts or separating connected components in an image.

### 2. Dilation

- **Definition:** Dilation adds pixels to the edges of objects, effectively growing or expanding the objects. It sets a pixel in the output image to 1 if any pixel under the structuring element in the input image is 1.
- **How It Works:** As the structuring element moves across the image, pixels in the structuring element that overlap with object pixels cause the corresponding pixel in the output to be set to 1.
- **Effects:** Expands the objects, fills in small holes or gaps, and can connect close objects.
- **Applications:** Dilation is used to fill in gaps within objects, connect broken parts, or make objects more prominent.

### 3. Opening

- **Definition:** Opening is an operation that involves applying erosion followed by dilation, using the same structuring element for both steps.

- **Effects:** Removes small objects or noise and smooths the contour of larger objects without significantly affecting their size.
- **Applications:** Often used for noise reduction, such as removing small specks or smoothing the edges of objects.

## 4. Closing

- **Definition:** Closing involves applying dilation followed by erosion, using the same structuring element for both steps.
  - **Effects:** Fills small holes or gaps within objects and smooths their boundaries.
- **Applications:** Closing is useful for filling gaps or connecting disjointed parts of objects, which is valuable in tasks like text processing or filling minor breaks in object boundaries.

## 5. Hit-or-Miss Transformation

- **Definition:** The hit-or-miss transformation detects specific patterns or shapes within a binary image by using two structuring elements: one for the foreground and another for the background.
- **How It Works:** The transformation searches for a specific configuration of pixels (both 1s and 0s) that match the pattern of the structuring elements.
- **Applications:** Used for detecting specific shapes or patterns within an image, such as corners, lines, or other predefined structures.

## Compound Morphological Operations

Morphological operations can be combined to create more complex effects or to analyze specific structures within binary images.

- **Morphological Gradient:** The difference between a dilated image and an eroded image. It highlights the edges of objects, useful for boundary detection. $\text{Gradient} = \text{Dilation}(A) - \text{Erosion}(A)$
- **Top-Hat Transform:** The difference between the original image and the opened image. It highlights small objects or structures that are smaller than the structuring element. $\text{Top-Hat} = A - \text{Opening}(A)$
- **Bottom-Hat Transform:** The difference between the closed image and the original image. It highlights dark structures on a bright background. $\text{Bottom-Hat} = \text{Closing}(A) - A$

## Applications of Binary Morphology

- **Noise Reduction:** Removing small, isolated pixels or artifacts from images.
- **Shape Analysis:** Analyzing and refining shapes of objects, useful in medical imaging, industrial inspection, and microscopy.
- **Object Detection and Counting:** Identifying, isolating, and counting specific objects in an image, such as cells in biomedical imaging or particles in material science.
- **Image Segmentation:** Separating distinct regions or components within an image, particularly for preprocessing in more complex computer vision tasks.

Binary morphology is essential for refining and analyzing shapes within binary images, forming a core part of many image processing pipelines.

# Colour image processing

Color image processing involves techniques and algorithms designed specifically for processing color images, where each pixel contains color information in addition to brightness or intensity. This form of processing is widely used in fields like digital photography, computer vision, medical imaging, and multimedia. Understanding how to work with color information opens up possibilities for enhanced image analysis, object recognition, and various applications that rely on color differentiation.

## Basics of Color Representation

Color images are typically represented as a combination of three primary color channels (Red, Green, and Blue - RGB), but other color models like HSV, YCbCr, and CMYK are also used for specific purposes. Each color model has its advantages depending on the type of processing required.

- **RGB (Red, Green, Blue):** The most common color model, used in digital screens and cameras. Each pixel is represented by three values, corresponding to the intensities of red, green, and blue.
- **HSV (Hue, Saturation, Value):** Separates color information (hue) from brightness (value) and purity (saturation), which can be useful for tasks like object tracking and segmentation.
- **YCbCr:** A color model often used in image compression and video encoding, where Y represents luminance (brightness), and Cb and Cr represent chrominance (color information).
- **CMYK (Cyan, Magenta, Yellow, Key/Black):** Primarily used in printing, where colors are produced through a subtractive process.

## Key Techniques in Color Image Processing

### 1. Color Transformation and Conversion

- **Definition:** Color transformations involve converting an image from one color space to another to facilitate specific types of processing. For example, RGB images can be converted to HSV for easier segmentation based on color.
- **Applications:** Useful for color-based object detection (e.g., tracking a red ball), where converting to HSV allows for isolating the color information from the intensity, making the object easier to detect.

### 2. Histogram Equalization for Color Images

- **Definition:** Histogram equalization enhances the contrast of an image by redistributing pixel intensities. In color images, this is often applied to the luminance channel (e.g., Y channel in YCbCr or V in HSV) to avoid distorting the colors.
- **Applications:** Improves the visual contrast of color images, making them look sharper and more vivid. Commonly used in digital photo enhancement.

### 3. Color Filtering and Color Segmentation

- **Definition:** Color filtering or segmentation is the process of isolating parts of an image based on specific color values. By setting thresholds on certain color channels, it's possible to separate objects or regions based on color.

- **Example:** In an RGB image, a red filter might retain only areas with high red values and low blue/green values, making it effective for isolating red objects.
- **Applications:** Color segmentation is commonly used in object tracking, medical imaging, and traffic sign detection, where specific colors (like red or green) are critical for identifying relevant regions.

### 4. Color Balance and White Balance

- **Definition:** Adjusts the color balance in an image to remove color casts and improve color accuracy. White balance corrects the image so that objects that appear white in real life also appear white in the image.
- **Applications:** Essential in photography and video to achieve natural-looking images under varying lighting conditions. Adjusting white balance is especially useful in scenes lit by artificial light sources with different color temperatures.

### 5. False Color and Pseudocolor Processing

- **Definition:** False color or pseudocolor processing assigns arbitrary colors to grayscale images based on intensity values. This is common in scientific and medical imaging where grayscale values represent specific data ranges.
- **Applications:** Used in thermal imaging, satellite imaging, and medical scans (e.g., MRI) to visually distinguish between intensity ranges, which can make it easier to identify structures or abnormalities.

### 6. Color-Based Edge Detection

- **Definition:** Color edge detection identifies edges within each color channel (R, G, B) separately or through the luminance channel, detecting boundaries where there is a significant color change.
- **Techniques:** Standard edge detectors (e.g., Sobel, Canny) can be applied to each color channel independently, and the results are combined, or edge detection can be applied on the intensity channel in other color spaces.
- **Applications:** Used in object recognition and segmentation tasks where object boundaries are defined by color changes.

### 7. Color Image Smoothing and Sharpening

- **Definition:** Smoothing and sharpening techniques are applied separately to each color channel, as processing all channels together can lead to color distortion. Gaussian or median filters can be used for noise reduction, while Laplacian or unsharp masking techniques enhance edges.
- **Applications:** These techniques improve image quality by reducing noise and enhancing details, especially in photography and computer vision applications.

### Advanced Applications in Color Image Processing

### 1. Color Constancy

- **Description:** Color constancy algorithms adjust images to ensure colors remain consistent under different lighting conditions, aiming to make the colors appear natural. This is achieved by estimating and

compensating for the light source in an image.
- **Applications:** Used in camera systems, computer vision, and augmented reality to maintain color accuracy across various environments.

## 2. Image Segmentation Based on Color Clustering

- **Description:** Clustering algorithms (like K-means or Gaussian Mixture Models) group pixels based on color similarities, allowing objects or regions to be separated based on their colors.
- **Applications:** Useful in applications like object recognition and medical imaging, where color is a key feature for identifying and segmenting regions.

## 3. Color Image Compression

- **Description:** Color images contain more data than grayscale images, making compression essential. Techniques like JPEG compression are commonly applied to color images, often reducing color information in chrominance channels more than in the luminance channel, as the human eye is less sensitive to color variations.
- **Applications:** Essential for reducing file sizes in digital media, web images, and video streaming.

## Challenges in Color Image Processing

- **Color Variability:** Differences in lighting and environmental conditions can affect color consistency, making accurate processing more challenging.
- **Computational Complexity:** Color images have more data than grayscale images, requiring more memory and processing power.
- **Color Perception:** Human color perception is subjective, and color-based algorithms may need to consider perceptual color models (like Lab) to ensure visually accurate results.

Color image processing techniques allow for sophisticated analysis and manipulation of images where color plays a critical role, enabling diverse applications across fields like medicine, photography, industrial inspection, and computer vision.

# 2 Mark Questions

### Machine Vision Software

1. Define machine vision software.
2. List two applications of machine vision software.
3. What is the role of imaging libraries in machine vision software?
4. How is pattern recognition used in machine vision?

### Fundamentals of Digital Image

1. Define a digital image.
2. What is image resolution, and how is it measured?
3. Describe the RGB color model.
4. What is bit depth in digital images?

### Image Acquisition Modes

1. What is single image acquisition mode?
2. Describe the difference between time-lapse acquisition and burst mode acquisition.
3. What is triggered acquisition, and where is it used?
4. Explain the concept of multi-spectral acquisition.

### Image Processing in Spatial and Frequency Domain

1. Differentiate between spatial domain and frequency domain processing.
2. What is the purpose of the Fourier Transform in image processing?
3. Give an example of a filtering operation in the spatial domain.
4. Explain the purpose of low-pass filtering in the frequency domain.

### Point Operation, Thresholding, Grayscale Stretching

1. What is a point operation in image processing?
2. Define thresholding in image processing.
3. Explain grayscale stretching.
4. How does thresholding aid in image segmentation?

### Neighborhood Operations, Image Smoothing, and Sharpening

1. Define a neighborhood operation.
2. How does Gaussian filtering help in image smoothing?
3. What is the purpose of image sharpening?
4. Name two common techniques used for image smoothing.

### Edge Detection

1. What is edge detection?
2. Differentiate between the Sobel and Canny edge detectors.
3. How does edge detection help in object recognition?
4. What is the purpose of gradient calculation in edge detection?

## Binary Morphology

1. Define binary morphology.
2. Describe the process of erosion in binary morphology.
3. What is the difference between opening and closing in morphological operations?
4. Give an example of how binary morphology is used in noise reduction.

## Colour Image Processing

1. What is the HSV color model?
2. Define color segmentation.
3. Explain the purpose of white balance in color image processing.
4. What is the purpose of false color processing?

# 15 Mark Questions

## Machine Vision Software

1. Explain the architecture of machine vision software. Discuss its key components, including imaging libraries, machine learning models, and user interface tools, and elaborate on how they contribute to industrial automation.
2. Describe in detail the applications of machine vision software in quality inspection, robotics, and object recognition. Provide examples to illustrate how machine vision software is implemented in real-world scenarios.

## Fundamentals of Digital Image

1. Explain the structure of a digital image in terms of pixels, resolution, and bit depth. Discuss how these factors affect image quality and storage requirements, and illustrate with examples.
2. Compare and contrast different color models used in digital imaging (RGB, HSV, CMYK, and YCbCr). Discuss the advantages and limitations of each model in various image processing applications.

## Image Acquisition Modes

1. Describe various image acquisition modes (single, continuous, triggered, time-lapse, burst mode, multi-spectral, and line-scan). Compare their applications, advantages, and limitations in fields like manufacturing, medical imaging, and surveillance.
2. Explain in detail the stereo or 3D imaging acquisition mode. Discuss the principles behind 3D imaging, its applications in autonomous vehicles and robotics, and the challenges involved in implementing this mode.

## Image Processing in Spatial and Frequency Domain

1. Differentiate between image processing in the spatial domain and the frequency domain. Explain how each domain is used for image enhancement, and provide examples of filtering techniques used in both domains.
2. Describe the Fourier Transform and its significance in frequency domain processing. Explain how low-pass and high-pass filtering are applied in the frequency domain, and discuss their impact on image quality.

## Point Operation, Thresholding, Grayscale Stretching

1. Describe point operations in image processing, including brightness and contrast adjustment. Explain the importance of thresholding and grayscale stretching in enhancing images and discuss how they are applied in different applications.
2. Explain the concept of thresholding in detail. Discuss various thresholding techniques (global, adaptive, and Otsu's method) and their applications in image segmentation, using examples.

## Neighborhood Operations, Image Smoothing, and Sharpening

1. Describe neighborhood operations in image processing. Explain the role of image smoothing (e.g., mean, median, and Gaussian filtering) and sharpening (e.g., Laplacian and unsharp masking) in enhancing image quality, and discuss their applications.
2. Explain the difference between image smoothing and sharpening. Discuss the various filters used for each, their mathematical basis, and provide examples of applications where each technique is essential.

## Edge Detection

1. Explain the concept of edge detection in image processing. Compare different edge detection techniques (e.g., Sobel, Prewitt, Laplacian of Gaussian, and Canny) in terms of their effectiveness, complexity, and applications.
2. Describe the Canny edge detection algorithm in detail. Discuss its multi-step process, including Gaussian smoothing, gradient calculation, non-maximum suppression, double thresholding, and edge tracking by hysteresis, and explain why it is widely used in computer vision.

## Binary Morphology

1. Describe binary morphology and its significance in image processing. Explain key morphological operations like erosion, dilation, opening, and closing, and discuss their applications in object detection, noise reduction, and image segmentation.
2. Explain the hit-or-miss transformation in binary morphology. Discuss how it is used to detect specific shapes or patterns within a binary image and give examples of applications where this transformation is beneficial.

## Colour Image Processing

1. Describe color image processing and explain the importance of color spaces like RGB and HSV. Discuss color-based image segmentation and its applications in fields like medical imaging and object tracking, providing examples.
2. Explain color constancy and white balance in color image processing. Discuss their importance in maintaining color accuracy across different lighting conditions, and provide examples of how they are used in photography and computer vision.

# CHAPTER FOUR

# FEATURE EXTRACTION

Feature extraction – Region Features, Shape and Size features – Texture Analysis – Template Matching and Classification – 3D Machine Vision Techniques – Decision Making.

# Feature extraction

In image processing, feature extraction is crucial for identifying and isolating the unique, informative parts of an image that can be used for tasks like object recognition, classification, and segmentation. By reducing an image's data to key elements, feature extraction techniques enable models to detect patterns more efficiently without unnecessary detail.

**Key Aspects of Feature Extraction in Image Processing**

Image features can capture specific characteristics like shape, texture, edges, and color. Here are some widely-used types of features in image processing:

**Color Features:**

- Color is often the most basic feature, and it's represented in spaces like RGB (Red, Green, Blue) or HSV (Hue, Saturation, Value).
- Color histograms quantify the distribution of colors in an image, which can be helpful for image retrieval tasks and similarity matching.

**Shape Features:**

- Shape features describe an object's outline or structure. These can include specific shapes (circles, rectangles) or more abstract descriptors.
  - Contours represent the boundaries of objects and are used for tracking object shapes.
- Edge detection methods like the Sobel or Canny edge detectors highlight the boundaries within an image, allowing the identification of object outlines.

**Texture Features:**

- Texture provides information about the surface characteristics of an object within an image, such as smoothness, roughness, or patterns.
- **Haralick Features (or Gray-Level Co-occurrence Matrix - GLCM):** Extracts textural characteristics like contrast, correlation, and homogeneity, which describe how pixel intensities relate spatially.
  - **Local Binary Patterns (LBP):** A method that considers the surrounding pixels to generate a binary representation, capturing textures effectively for face and pattern recognition tasks.

**Keypoints and Descriptors:**

- Keypoints are points of interest in an image, like corners or blobs, and descriptors describe the characteristics around these keypoints.
- Scale-Invariant Feature Transform (SIFT) and Speeded Up Robust Features (SURF): These extract and describe local features that remain consistent under transformations like scaling or rotation. They're highly effective in object recognition and image stitching.
- Oriented FAST and Rotated BRIEF (ORB): A faster alternative to SIFT and SURF, it's often used in real-time applications.

## Histogram of Oriented Gradients (HOG):

- HOG is widely used in object detection, especially for identifying humans. It divides an image into cells, computes the gradient orientation histogram for each cell, and combines these histograms to describe the object's structure.

## Wavelet Transform:

- The wavelet transform decomposes an image into different frequency components, capturing both high-frequency details and low-frequency shapes. This is used in applications like image compression and texture analysis.

## Fourier Transform:

- Fourier transforms break down an image into its frequency components, capturing patterns and textures. This can be useful for image denoising and certain texture recognition tasks.

## Applications of Feature Extraction in Image Processing

- **Object Detection and Recognition:** Extracted features like edges, shapes, and keypoints are used in identifying objects, such as faces or cars.
- **Image Classification:** Classifying images based on their content, where color, texture, and shape features often play a key role.
- **Image Matching and Retrieval:** Image databases often use feature descriptors to compare and retrieve similar images.
- **Medical Imaging:** Features extracted from MRI or X-ray images help in identifying anomalies like tumors.
- **Facial Recognition:** Keypoints and descriptors are used to recognize facial features, which has applications in security and social media.

## Workflow of Feature Extraction in Image Processing

- **Preprocessing:** Images are often converted to grayscale or resized to make computation easier.
- **Feature Extraction:** Techniques like edge detection, keypoint detection, or texture analysis are applied to capture essential aspects of the image.
- **Feature Representation:** Features are organized into vectors, histograms, or matrices.
- **Model Training or Matching:** These features are then used in machine learning models or compared against other images in databases for various tasks.

Feature extraction in image processing is essential because it condenses information from pixels into meaningful patterns, significantly enhancing the ability of algorithms to recognize, classify, and make inferences from visual data.

# Region Features, Shape and Size features

Region, shape, and size features are critical in image processing for analyzing and understanding the structure, geometry, and spatial relationships of objects within an image. Here's a breakdown of each:

## 1. Region Features

Region features focus on properties within a specified area or segment of an image, often an object or a particular region of interest (ROI). These features help capture characteristics of a region, such as intensity, color, and texture.

### Key types of region features include:

- **Intensity and Color Statistics:** The mean, median, variance, or histogram of pixel intensities or colors in a region, which provides insights into the brightness or color distribution.
- **Texture Descriptors:** Describes the texture within a region, such as smoothness, coarseness, or regularity, using methods like GLCM (Gray-Level Co-occurrence Matrix), LBP (Local Binary Pattern), and Haralick features.
- **Moment-Based Descriptors:** Moments (like raw moments, central moments, and Hu moments) describe the spatial distribution of pixel intensities. These are often invariant to transformations like translation and rotation, making them valuable for identifying specific objects in images.

Applications of region features include object detection, image segmentation, and analyzing localized patterns, such as textures in skin cancer detection or anomaly detection in industrial images.

## 2. Shape Features

Shape features characterize the geometric structure and contours of an object within an image. They are particularly useful for recognizing or differentiating objects based on their form.

### Important shape features include:

- **Perimeter:** The length of the boundary around the object, often calculated using contour extraction methods.
- **Convex Hull:** The smallest convex shape that can enclose a region or object, often used to measure the convexity and compactness of an object.
- **Eccentricity:** A measure of how elongated an object is. It's the ratio of the distance between the foci of the ellipse that best fits the object and the length of its major axis, providing insight into an object's roundness.
- **Aspect Ratio:** The ratio of width to height, useful for distinguishing between elongated and compact objects.
- **Solidity:** Calculated as the area of the object divided by the area of its convex hull. It measures how solid or convex the object is.
- **Contour Descriptors:** Approximations of an object's boundary, like Fourier Descriptors or Shape Context, capture the object's shape and are invariant to transformations like scaling, translation, and rotation.

Applications of shape features include object recognition, logo identification, character recognition, and tracking objects that have a unique shape, such as license plates or fingerprints.

### 3. Size Features

Size features measure the physical dimensions or area of an object within an image. They provide scale information, which can be crucial for tasks requiring spatial measurements or size-based categorization.

Primary size features include:

- **Area:** The number of pixels within a region. It's a straightforward measure of an object's size and can be used to filter out small, irrelevant regions in images.
- **Bounding Box:** The smallest rectangle that can contain the object. Properties like the width, height, and aspect ratio of the bounding box are often used in detecting and categorizing objects.
- **Major and Minor Axes:** For ellipsoidal objects, these refer to the longest and shortest diameters. They provide a way to understand the orientation and size of elongated objects.
- **EquivDiameter (Equivalent Diameter):** The diameter of a circle with the same area as the object, which provides a circular approximation of an object's size.

Applications of size features include counting and classifying objects (like counting cells in biomedical images), filtering regions based on their size, and analyzing relative object sizes, which is common in satellite imaging and agricultural applications.

Applications and Usage

- **Object Detection and Recognition:** Shape and size features are crucial for detecting specific objects like vehicles, animals, or faces, and differentiating them based on geometry.
- **Image Segmentation:** Region features are widely used for segmenting parts of an image, especially in medical imaging for identifying tumors or other regions of interest.
- **Quality Control in Manufacturing:** Size and shape features help detect irregularities in objects, such as scratches or deformations, based on their shape and area.
- **Image Retrieval:** In content-based image retrieval, region and shape features enable efficient matching of objects in a database based on form and size.

By leveraging these features, image processing models can make sense of object geometry, spatial relationships, and localized properties, making it possible to recognize, classify, and analyze objects accurately and efficiently.

# Texture Analysis

Texture analysis in image processing is the study of the visual patterns in an image that describe the surface characteristics of objects, such as roughness, smoothness, granularity, or regularity. Texture analysis is crucial in applications where the surface properties of objects are important, such as in medical imaging (for detecting tissue anomalies), satellite image classification (for distinguishing land types), and industrial quality control.

## Key Concepts in Texture Analysis

Textures are defined by the spatial distribution of pixel intensities in an image and can be characterized by:

1. **Statistical Properties:** Describing textures by the distribution of intensity values (like roughness, smoothness).
2. **Structural Properties:** Defining textures as repetitive patterns or primitives.
3. **Spectral Properties:** Using frequency information to capture periodic or random patterns.

## Techniques for Texture Analysis

### Statistical Methods

Statistical methods analyze the spatial distribution of gray-level values. They are effective in capturing random textures and are widely used for texture-based segmentation and classification.

### Gray-Level Co-occurrence Matrix (GLCM):

- GLCM describes how often pairs of pixel with specific values occur in a certain spatial relationship within an image. From the GLCM, features such as contrast, homogeneity, energy, and correlation can be computed.
  - These features provide insights into the texture's roughness, regularity, and directionality.

### Local Binary Patterns (LBP):

- LBP is a simple and efficient method for texture description. It converts pixel neighborhoods into binary codes based on comparing each pixel to its neighbors.
- LBP is effective in distinguishing fine textures, such as in face recognition, where it captures details of the skin's texture.

### Higher-Order Statistics (e.g., Laws' Texture Energy):

- These methods use energy masks to capture localized texture properties in an image. By applying different filters, specific texture patterns (like ripples, waves, or lines) can be identified.

### Transform-Based Methods

- Transform-based methods analyze textures by converting the image data into the frequency domain, capturing repetitive patterns, directionality, and periodicity.

**Fourier Transform:**

- The Fourier transform decomposes the image into its frequency components, making it useful for detecting periodic textures and patterns.
- Textures with certain orientations or frequencies appear as distinct patterns in the frequency domain, which can help separate them from other textures.

**Wavelet Transform:**

- The wavelet transform captures both spatial and frequency information, making it suitable for textures that vary across scales.
- Wavelets are particularly effective in applications where multi-scale analysis is required, such as in medical imaging or geological applications.

**Gabor Filters:**

- Gabor filters are frequency-based filters that are highly effective for capturing textures that have specific orientations and scales.
- These filters are commonly used in texture segmentation, feature extraction, and edge detection due to their ability to analyze localized texture variations in specific orientations.

**Model-Based Methods**

- Model-based methods attempt to model the texture statistically, often with random field models.

**Markov Random Fields (MRF):**

- MRF models the spatial relationship between pixels in a neighborhood, capturing texture patterns based on local interactions.
- MRF is effective in representing complex textures and is used in image segmentation and synthesis tasks.

**Fractal Analysis:**

- Fractal analysis quantifies texture based on the self-similarity and complexity of textures across scales, often described with a "fractal dimension."
- Fractals are useful for textures that exhibit a high degree of self-similarity, such as natural scenes, landscapes, and biological textures.

**Deep Learning-Based Methods**

- In recent years, deep learning methods have been applied to texture analysis, often through convolutional neural networks (CNNs).
- CNNs can automatically learn texture features by extracting hierarchical patterns, making them suitable for complex texture classification and segmentation tasks.
- Pretrained models on large datasets can also be fine-tuned for specific texture analysis applications, making deep learning methods adaptable to various domains.

## Applications of Texture Analysis

- **Medical Imaging:** Texture features help identify abnormalities, such as tumors, by analyzing the texture patterns of tissues. For instance, textures of tumor cells often differ from healthy tissues.
- **Remote Sensing and Satellite Imaging:** Texture analysis distinguishes between land cover types, like forests, water bodies, and urban areas, based on their distinct textures.
- **Quality Control:** In manufacturing, texture analysis detects surface defects or irregularities in products, such as cracks or scratches.
- **Document Analysis:** Textures in document images (like paper texture, ink spread) can be used to detect forgeries or analyze document age.
- **Biometric Recognition:** Texture patterns in fingerprints, faces, and irises provide unique identifiers for biometric recognition.

## Workflow for Texture Analysis

- **Preprocessing:** Images may be resized, converted to grayscale, or enhanced to highlight texture details.
- **Feature Extraction:** Apply texture extraction methods (e.g., GLCM, LBP, wavelets) to capture relevant texture features.
- **Feature Selection:** Select the most informative texture features based on the specific application, which helps improve model performance and reduce complexity.
- **Classification or Segmentation:** Use extracted texture features in a machine learning or deep learning model to classify or segment textures based on patterns.

## Summary

Texture analysis enables computers to understand and interpret the visual "feel" of surfaces, which is essential for a variety of applications that rely on recognizing fine-grained patterns and details. Different techniques provide unique perspectives on textures, making it possible to capture both micro-level details and large-scale spatial distributions in images.

# Template matching and classification

Template matching and classification are fundamental techniques in image processing, used for identifying and categorizing objects within images. Each has a unique approach to solving the problem of object detection, recognition, and classification in images, with template matching focused on matching specific patterns and classification centered around learning and recognizing patterns from training data.

## Template Matching

Template matching is a technique used to find and locate an object or pattern within an image by comparing a "template" (a smaller image or shape) against sections of a larger image. It's commonly used for tasks where the object of interest is expected to have a known and relatively invariant appearance.

### How Template Matching Works

1. **Template Selection:** A reference template, which is a cropped image or pre-defined pattern, is chosen. This template represents the object or pattern of interest.
2. **Sliding Window Comparison:** The template is slid over the image, comparing the template to every possible position in the target image. For each position, a similarity metric (like correlation) is calculated.
3. **Similarity Metrics:** Commonly used similarity metrics include:

- **Normalized Cross-Correlation (NCC):** Measures the similarity between the template and the overlapping region in the image, taking into account the template and image intensities.
- Sum of Absolute Differences (SAD): Computes the absolute differences in pixel values between the template and the overlapping area.
- Sum of Squared Differences (SSD): Computes the squared differences in pixel values, giving more weight to larger differences.

1. **Match Identification:** After evaluating the similarity across all positions, the best match corresponds to the highest similarity (or lowest difference) score, which indicates where the template is most likely located in the image.

### Applications of Template Matching

- **Object Detection:** Recognizing predefined shapes, such as logos, signs, or specific parts in industrial applications.
- **Facial Feature Detection:** Detecting specific facial features (like eyes or noses) in controlled environments.
- **Optical Character Recognition (OCR):** Recognizing printed characters by comparing them to template characters.
- **Medical Imaging:** Identifying anatomical structures, such as cells or organs, by matching known shapes within scan images.

### Limitations of Template Matching

- **Invariance Issues:** Template matching is sensitive to variations in scale, rotation, and illumination, so it works best when the target object appears with minimal variation.
- **Computationally Intensive:** Sliding the template over the entire image and calculating similarity for each position can be computationally expensive, especially for large images.

## Classification

Classification in image processing involves categorizing objects in an image into different classes or categories based on learned patterns. It typically uses machine learning or deep learning models trained on labeled data to recognize features within images and predict the class to which an object belongs.

### How Classification Works

1. **Data Collection:** A dataset of labeled images is collected. Each image is associated with a label (class) that defines what the image represents.
2. **Feature Extraction:** Key features of each image are extracted using methods like edge detection, color histograms, texture analysis, or, in modern techniques, feature extraction is handled by deep learning models.
3. **Model Training:** A classification algorithm (such as a neural network, decision tree, or support vector machine) is trained on the labeled dataset. The model learns to map extracted features to their corresponding classes.
4. **Prediction:** For a new, unlabeled image, the trained model extracts features, applies learned weights, and outputs a prediction for the image's class.

### Types of Classification Techniques

### Traditional Machine Learning Approaches:

- **K-Nearest Neighbors (KNN):** Classifies based on the classes of the closest examples in the feature space.
- **Support Vector Machine (SVM):** Separates classes by finding a hyperplane that maximally separates the data points in feature space.
- **Random Forests:** Uses an ensemble of decision trees to make classification decisions based on the majority vote of the trees.

### Deep Learning Approaches:

- **Convolutional Neural Networks (CNNs):** CNNs are specifically designed for image data, with convolutional layers that automatically learn and extract features like edges, shapes, and complex textures.
- **Transfer Learning:** Pretrained models (like VGG, ResNet, or Inception) are fine-tuned for specific classification tasks, significantly reducing training time and improving accuracy.

### Applications of Classification in Image Processing

- **Object Recognition:** Identifying and labeling objects in images, useful in applications like autonomous vehicles, security, and retail.

- **Face Recognition:** Classifying individuals based on facial features for security and authentication systems.
- **Medical Diagnosis:** Classifying medical images, such as MRIs or X-rays, to identify diseases or conditions.
- **Document Analysis:** Classifying document types, page layouts, or handwritten characters in scanned documents.

### Limitations of Classification

- **Need for Large, Labeled Datasets:** Accurate classification models often require large amounts of labeled training data, which can be challenging and costly to obtain.
- **Overfitting:** When models learn too much from training data, they may perform poorly on new data. Regularization and careful tuning are necessary to avoid overfitting.
- **Computational Resources:** Deep learning models, especially CNNs, can be computationally intensive, requiring high-powered GPUs and considerable memory.

### Comparison: Template Matching vs. Classification

- Template Matching is generally used when the object has a fixed and known appearance, making it suitable for tasks with minimal variation in scale, orientation, or lighting. It's often a simpler, faster approach for highly controlled environments.
- Classification offers greater flexibility and can generalize to varied, complex patterns, making it ideal for scenarios with variability and diverse object types. While more resource-intensive, it is better suited for dynamic applications where objects may appear in different sizes, orientations, and lighting conditions.

### Summary

Template matching and classification are both essential tools in image processing, serving different types of detection and recognition tasks. Template matching is ideal for simple, invariant matching tasks, while classification provides a robust solution for complex object recognition in diverse conditions.

# 3D machine vision techniques

3D machine vision techniques extend traditional 2D vision methods by capturing depth information, which provides a complete three-dimensional understanding of objects and scenes. This added depth dimension enables more accurate measurements, object recognition, surface inspection, and spatial analysis, especially in applications requiring precise positioning, orientation, and size detection. Here's an overview of the main 3D machine vision techniques and their applications.

## Key 3D Machine Vision Techniques

### Stereoscopic Vision (Stereo Vision)

- **Principle:** Stereo vision mimics human binocular vision by using two cameras positioned at different angles. By capturing images from slightly different viewpoints, the technique calculates depth based on the disparity (difference in positions) between corresponding points in the two images.

**Process:**

1. **Image Capture:** Two cameras capture images of the same scene from different angles.
2. **Image Matching:** Key points in the images are matched to find corresponding points.
3. **Depth Calculation:** Depth is calculated based on the disparity between corresponding points and the known distance between the cameras.

**Applications:** Stereoscopic vision is widely used in autonomous vehicles, robotic navigation, and industrial quality control, where spatial positioning and object distance measurement are important.

### Structured Light

**Principle:** A known pattern (e.g., stripes, dots, grids) of light is projected onto an object, and a camera captures the resulting deformation in the pattern caused by the object's surface. The distortion provides depth information about the object's surface.

**Process:**

1. **Pattern Projection:** A projector emits a structured light pattern onto the object.
2. **Image Capture:** A camera records how the pattern deforms over the object's surface.
3. **Depth Calculation:** By analyzing the deformation, the system calculates the 3D shape of the object.

**Applications:** Structured light is highly accurate and is commonly used in 3D scanning, facial recognition, and quality inspection in manufacturing (e.g., inspecting complex parts for defects).

### Time-of-Flight (ToF) Sensors

**Principle:** Time-of-flight sensors measure the time it takes for a light pulse, often infrared, to travel from the sensor to an object and back. This travel time is directly related to the distance, allowing the sensor to calculate the depth.

**Process:**

1. **Pulse Emission:** A sensor emits a pulse of light toward the object.
2. **Reflection Capture:** The sensor detects the reflected pulse and measures the time it took to return.
3. **Distance Calculation:** Using the speed of light, the system calculates the object's distance.

**Applications:** ToF sensors are widely used in gesture recognition, autonomous navigation, and AR/VR applications, where they provide fast, real-time 3D data.

### Laser Triangulation

**Principle:** Laser triangulation uses a laser beam projected onto an object and a camera to capture the laser dot or line. The position of the laser's reflection on the object relative to the camera indicates the object's distance.

**Process:**

1. **Laser Projection:** A laser projects a dot or line onto the object's surface.
2. **Image Capture:** A camera captures the reflection of the laser beam.
3. **Distance Calculation:** The distance is calculated based on the laser reflection's position in the camera image.

**Applications:** Laser triangulation is frequently used for high-precision measurements, such as in industrial inspection, surface profiling, and 3D reconstruction of small or complex parts.

### Photometric Stereo

**Principle:** Photometric stereo uses multiple images of the same object captured under different lighting conditions. By analyzing shading variations, it calculates the surface normals and creates a depth map of the object.

**Process:**

1. **Image Capture:** Multiple images of the object are taken, each with lighting from different directions.
2. **Shading Analysis:** The shading differences across the images are analyzed to determine surface normals.
3. **Depth Reconstruction:** Using surface normals, the depth information is inferred, creating a 3D representation.

**Applications:** Photometric stereo is useful in applications requiring detailed surface information, such as inspecting fine textures, material surface analysis, and identifying small defects in materials.

### Shape from Shading

**Principle:** Shape from shading analyzes the shading of a single image to infer the shape and depth information of an object. It assumes that variations in shading result from the 3D structure and lighting conditions.

**Process:**

- **Shading Capture:** An image of the object is captured under known lighting conditions.
  - **Shading Analysis:** Shading gradients are analyzed to estimate surface orientation.
  - **Depth Estimation:** Using orientation data, a 3D shape of the object is reconstructed.

**Applications:** Shape from shading is used for simple objects with smooth surfaces, commonly applied in fields like archaeology (for artifact reconstruction) and in forensic imaging.

## Volumetric Techniques (CT and MRI in Medical Imaging)

**Principle:** Volumetric techniques, such as computed tomography (CT) and magnetic resonance imaging (MRI), use multiple 2D cross-sectional images from different angles. These images are stacked to create a 3D model.

### Process:

1. **Image Acquisition:** 2D cross-sectional images are captured from various angles.
2. **Reconstruction:** The images are combined to create a 3D volume of the scanned area.

**Applications:** Volumetric techniques are widely used in medical imaging for detailed anatomical studies, tumor detection, and surgical planning.

## Applications of 3D Machine Vision

- **Automated Quality Control:** 3D vision systems inspect manufactured parts, measuring dimensions and identifying defects, which is essential in industries like automotive and electronics.
- **Autonomous Navigation:** Autonomous vehicles and drones use 3D machine vision for obstacle detection, path planning, and object recognition.
- **Robotic Guidance:** Robots rely on 3D vision for precise placement and handling of objects, essential in assembly lines and warehouse automation.
- **Biometric Recognition:** 3D facial recognition provides accurate identification by capturing depth details, improving security applications.
- **Medical Imaging:** 3D machine vision enhances diagnostic imaging, enabling non-invasive examination and aiding in procedures requiring spatial accuracy, such as surgery and tumor detection.

## Summary

3D machine vision techniques provide a richer perspective by capturing depth information, which is critical in environments where spatial understanding is essential. By selecting the appropriate technique, applications can benefit from highly accurate object detection, measurement, and recognition capabilities, enabling a broad range of use cases across industries.

# Decision making

Decision making in machine vision feature extraction refers to the process of interpreting and analyzing extracted features to reach conclusions about objects or scenes within an image. This decision-making process often follows feature extraction and is essential in guiding the final output, whether it's classifying an object, detecting defects, or identifying patterns. Here's how decision making fits within machine vision and the techniques typically used.

**Key Steps in Decision Making for Machine Vision**

### Feature Extraction:

- Raw data from images is processed to identify meaningful features, such as edges, textures, shapes, colors, or depth.
- Effective feature extraction simplifies the decision-making process by reducing the complexity of data and focusing on the most informative parts.

### Feature Selection:

- From the extracted features, the most relevant ones are selected to avoid redundancy and improve computational efficiency.
- Feature selection methods like Principal Component Analysis (PCA), Linear Discriminant Analysis (LDA), or filter-based approaches can reduce dimensionality and enhance decision accuracy.

### Classification and Pattern Recognition:

- Classification involves assigning objects or regions in an image to predefined classes or categories based on their features. Pattern recognition helps identify patterns and trends within the extracted features.
- Different algorithms, such as support vector machines (SVM), decision trees, k-nearest neighbors (KNN), or deep learning models (e.g., Convolutional Neural Networks or CNNs), are applied to make decisions based on the extracted features.

### Thresholding:

- Thresholding is a straightforward decision-making technique used to classify pixels or regions. A threshold value is set, and pixels or features are categorized based on whether they exceed this threshold.
- For instance, in defect detection, a brightness or texture threshold could separate defects from normal surfaces. Adaptive thresholding, where thresholds change based on local image properties, can also be used in more complex environments.

### Statistical Decision Making:

- Statistical decision-making models analyze features and assign probabilities to different classes, making decisions based on statistical confidence.
- Bayes' theorem, Gaussian mixture models, and Maximum Likelihood Estimation (MLE) are commonly used statistical methods, especially in applications where uncertainty or overlapping feature distributions

are present.

### Rule-Based Decision Making:

- In rule-based systems, a set of logical rules determines the decision based on feature values. This approach is useful when there is clear, domain-specific knowledge about the features.
- For example, in quality control, a rule might be "if the length is greater than X and width is less than Y, classify as defective." Rule-based decision making is often used for simpler, highly controlled tasks.

### Fuzzy Logic:

- Fuzzy logic is used when decision making involves ambiguous or imprecise data. It allows for degrees of membership in classes, rather than strict binary classifications.
- In machine vision, fuzzy logic helps make decisions in cases with unclear boundaries, such as determining the quality of materials with minor variations. Fuzzy rules are created to handle situations where exact feature thresholds are difficult to define.

### Machine Learning and Deep Learning Models:

Advanced machine vision systems often use machine learning (ML) and deep learning (DL) models to make complex decisions based on extracted features.

- **Machine Learning Models:** Algorithms like support vector machines (SVM), random forests, and k-nearest neighbors (KNN) learn from labeled data to make predictions. These are effective for moderately complex decisions and work well with structured features.
- **Deep Learning Models:** Convolutional neural networks (CNNs) and other deep architectures can automatically learn feature hierarchies, enabling them to make decisions directly from images without explicit feature extraction. These models excel in tasks like image classification, object detection, and pattern recognition, especially in applications with diverse, complex data.

### Ensemble Decision Making:

- Ensemble methods combine multiple models or decision rules to improve overall decision accuracy. Techniques like bagging, boosting, and voting use multiple classifiers to enhance performance and robustness.
- This approach is beneficial in complex scenarios, as it allows for multiple perspectives on the same data, reducing the likelihood of incorrect decisions.

### Applications of Decision Making in Machine Vision

- **Object Recognition:** Identifying and classifying objects within an image based on their features, useful in robotics, security, and manufacturing.
- **Quality Control:** Decision-making algorithms analyze features to detect defects, ensuring products meet quality standards in industries like automotive and electronics.
- **Medical Imaging:** Automated decision making helps in diagnosing conditions from features in scans, such as X-rays, MRIs, and CT images, enabling more accurate and consistent diagnostic processes.

- **Autonomous Vehicles:** Machine vision systems use decision-making models to recognize road signs, lane markings, and obstacles, supporting real-time navigation and safety decisions.
  - **Facial Recognition:** Features extracted from facial images (like landmarks and textures) are used to identify or verify individuals, commonly applied in security and biometrics.

### Workflow of Decision Making in Machine Vision

1. **Image Acquisition:** Capture images using cameras or sensors.
2. **Preprocessing:** Enhance images through noise reduction, normalization, or contrast adjustments to improve feature extraction accuracy.
3. **Feature Extraction and Selection:** Extract and select key features relevant to the decision-making task.
4. **Decision Model Training:** Train a decision model (e.g., ML, DL, rule-based) on labeled data to recognize patterns and make predictions.
5. **Prediction and Interpretation:** Use the model to analyze new images, interpret the predictions, and make decisions based on the outputs.
6. **Evaluation and Refinement:** Evaluate the decision-making accuracy and refine the model or rules to optimize performance, especially as new data becomes available.

### Summary

In machine vision, decision making after feature extraction is what enables actionable insights. The decision-making approach chosen—whether statistical, rule-based, or based on advanced ML and DL models—depends on the complexity of the task, data variability, and required accuracy. As a result, decision-making techniques are fundamental in translating raw visual data into valuable information for industrial automation, healthcare, security, and autonomous systems.

# 2 Mark Questions

### Feature Extraction

1. What is feature extraction, and why is it important in machine vision?
2. List two common techniques used in feature extraction.
3. Explain the role of feature selection in feature extraction.

### Region Features

1. What are region features in image processing?
2. Give two examples of region features used in image analysis.
3. How are intensity and color statistics used as region features?

### Shape and Size Features

1. Define shape features in image processing.
2. What is the role of aspect ratio in shape analysis?
3. Explain the use of the convex hull in shape feature analysis.

### Texture Analysis

1. What is texture analysis, and where is it commonly applied?
2. List two methods used for texture analysis in images.
3. How is the Gray-Level Co-occurrence Matrix (GLCM) used in texture analysis?

### Template Matching and Classification

1. What is template matching, and how is it applied in machine vision?
2. Differentiate between template matching and classification.
3. Explain the term "normalized cross-correlation" in template matching.

### 3D Machine Vision Techniques

1. What is stereoscopic vision, and how does it work?
2. Briefly explain the structured light technique in 3D machine vision.
3. Define time-of-flight sensors and their application in 3D vision.

### Decision Making

1. How is decision making applied in machine vision systems?
2. List two decision-making methods used after feature extraction.
3. What is thresholding in decision making, and give an example of its use.

# 15 Mark Questions

### Feature Extraction

1. Explain the process of feature extraction in machine vision. Discuss its importance in image processing and list various techniques used for feature extraction. Illustrate your answer with examples of how feature extraction impacts object recognition and classification tasks.

### Region Features

1. Define region features and describe their significance in image analysis. Explain the types of region features, including intensity and color statistics, texture descriptors, and moment-based features, with examples of how they are applied in different machine vision tasks.

### Shape and Size Features

1. Discuss shape and size features in detail and their applications in image processing. Explain the importance of perimeter, convex hull, aspect ratio, and bounding box in shape analysis. Provide examples to illustrate how these features assist in distinguishing objects in real-world applications.

### Texture Analysis

1. Define texture analysis and its role in machine vision. Describe various methods for analyzing texture, including Gray-Level Co-occurrence Matrix (GLCM), Local Binary Patterns (LBP), and Gabor filters. Include examples of where texture analysis is applied in industries like medical imaging, remote sensing, and manufacturing.

### Template Matching and Classification

1. Compare and contrast template matching and classification in machine vision. Explain the processes, techniques, and applications of both approaches, with emphasis on the advantages and limitations of each in different image processing scenarios. Provide examples to illustrate your answer.

### 3D Machine Vision Techniques

1. Describe various 3D machine vision techniques, including stereoscopic vision, structured light, time-of-flight sensors, and laser triangulation. Discuss their principles, processes, and applications in fields such as autonomous navigation, industrial quality control, and medical imaging. Provide examples where each technique is best suited.

### Decision Making in Machine Vision

1. Explain the role of decision making in machine vision after feature extraction. Discuss various decision-making techniques, such as thresholding, rule-based systems, fuzzy logic, and machine learning models, with examples of how they are applied in applications like object classification, defect detection, and pattern recognition.

# CHAPTER FIVE

# MACHINE VISION APPLICATIONS

Machine vision applications in manufacturing, electronics, printing, pharmaceutical, textile, applications in non-visible spectrum, metrology and gauging, OCR and OCV, vision guided robotics – Field and Service Applications – Agricultural, and Bio medical field, augmented reality, surveillance, bio-metrics.

# Machine vision applications in manufacturing

Machine vision is a vital technology in manufacturing, helping improve efficiency, accuracy, and quality control. It involves using cameras, sensors, and computer algorithms to inspect, analyze, and interpret visual data. Here are some key applications of machine vision in manufacturing:

## 1. Quality Inspection and Defect Detection

- Machine vision systems inspect products for defects (like cracks, scratches, or misalignment) on production lines. They offer high-speed and precise inspection, allowing defective products to be detected and removed before reaching consumers. This improves quality and reduces returns or warranty claims.

## 2. Dimensional Measurement and Gauging

- Automated measurement systems can gauge product dimensions and ensure they fall within specified tolerances. Machine vision ensures that each part meets the precise specifications, critical in industries like automotive and aerospace.

## 3. Guidance and Robotics Integration

- Vision-guided robots use machine vision to locate and handle objects, aiding in tasks like assembly, sorting, and pick-and-place operations. Machine vision allows robots to work more flexibly, adapting to varied shapes, sizes, and orientations of parts on the fly.

## 4. Barcode and QR Code Reading

- Machine vision enables automated reading and verification of barcodes, QR codes, and other optical markers. This capability is crucial for tracking products and materials throughout the production line, inventory management, and logistics.

## 5. Assembly Verification

- In assembly lines, machine vision systems verify that each component is correctly assembled and aligned. This helps reduce errors in complex assemblies, ensuring that all parts are in place and correctly oriented before moving to the next production stage.

## 6. Surface Inspection and Texture Analysis

- Vision systems analyze the surface texture of products for consistency and uniformity. For example, in industries like textiles, electronics, and automotive, machine vision can detect surface defects, such as scratches or discoloration.

## 7. Color and Pattern Matching

- Machine vision technology can identify specific colors and patterns, useful in applications like quality control of painted or printed products, textiles, and packaging. It ensures consistency and adherence to color and pattern specifications.

## 8. Sorting and Material Handling

- Machine vision systems enable automated sorting based on size, shape, color, and other visual attributes. For example, in the food and beverage industry, machine vision can sort fruits, vegetables, and other items based on their size and appearance.

## 9. OCR (Optical Character Recognition)

- OCR allows manufacturers to read and log serial numbers, batch numbers, and other text printed on products or packaging. This helps with traceability and compliance with regulatory requirements.

## 10. 3D Vision Applications

- 3D machine vision technology captures depth and volume information. This is beneficial in applications like measuring object volume, inspecting complex shapes, and guiding robots in picking and placing irregularly shaped objects.

### Benefits of Machine Vision in Manufacturing:

- **Accuracy and Consistency:** High precision reduces human error and variability in inspection and handling processes.
- **Speed and Efficiency:** Machine vision systems can operate 24/7 at high speeds, handling tasks much faster than human inspectors.
- **Data Collection and Analytics:** Captures data that can be analyzed for process improvements, predictive maintenance, and quality control.
- **Reduced Costs:** Automated inspection and handling reduce labor costs, minimize rework, and prevent losses from defective products reaching consumers.

Machine vision continues to evolve, with advancements in AI and deep learning enabling more complex and adaptive applications in the manufacturing field.

# Machine vision applications in electronics

Machine vision plays a crucial role in the electronics industry by ensuring high standards of precision, quality, and efficiency in various stages of production and quality control. Here's how it's applied:

### 1. PCB Inspection (Printed Circuit Board)

- Machine vision inspects PCBs to verify the placement and soldering of components. It checks for defects like missing or misplaced components, soldering errors, short circuits, and damaged circuits, ensuring each board meets stringent quality standards.
- It performs Optical Character Recognition (OCR) to read component markings and verify against design specs.

### 2. Assembly Verification

- Assembling electronics components, such as chipsets, resistors, capacitors, and transistors, requires high precision. Machine vision ensures correct component alignment and orientation, preventing assembly errors.
  - It also checks for proper connections and correct layering in devices with complex assemblies, like smartphones and laptops.

### 3. Surface Mount Technology (SMT) Inspection

- SMT is widely used for mounting electronic components onto PCBs. Machine vision checks the accuracy of SMT processes by verifying solder paste application, component alignment, and solder joint quality. This ensures components are precisely placed and soldered onto PCBs, reducing defects in high-density assemblies.

### 4. Display Inspection

- For devices with screens, such as smartphones, tablets, and TVs, machine vision checks for dead pixels, uniform brightness, color accuracy, and clarity. This helps maintain display quality by detecting issues early, ensuring consistent quality for end-users.

### 5. Connector and Pin Inspection

- Connectors and pins are essential for establishing electrical connections. Machine vision checks the position, alignment, and quality of connectors and pins, ensuring they're not bent, misaligned, or damaged. This reduces failures in connectivity in the final product.

### 6. Microelectronics Inspection

- In microelectronics, where components are extremely small, machine vision performs detailed inspection at microscopic levels. This includes chip surface inspection, wire bonding inspection, and even wafer inspection in semiconductor manufacturing to detect cracks, contamination, and other tiny defects.

## 7. Battery Inspection

- For electronics powered by batteries, machine vision inspects the battery cells and casings for physical defects. It can detect cracks, leaks, and other damage that could compromise battery safety and performance, essential for consumer electronics and electric vehicles (EVs).

## 8. Component Traceability

- Electronics manufacturing requires strict component traceability due to regulatory standards and quality assurance. Machine vision performs barcode, QR code, and OCR reading to track components and parts from suppliers through production to the final product. This enables efficient recalls and compliance with traceability standards.

## 9. Solder Joint Inspection

- Machine vision systems inspect solder joints for integrity and quality, crucial in ensuring solid connections between components and PCBs. It detects issues like cold solder joints, insufficient solder, and bridging between pins, improving the reliability of electronics.

## 10. Wire and Cable Inspection

- Machine vision inspects wiring and cables for proper length, alignment, color coding, and connections. It ensures correct assembly in complex electronics and prevents potential connectivity or grounding issues in the final product.

## 11. 3D Vision Applications in Electronics Assembly

- 3D vision allows for depth perception, which is essential for inspecting objects with complex geometries or multi-layered assemblies. This is particularly useful for inspecting components from different angles, improving the accuracy of inspection in high-precision electronics.

### Benefits of Machine Vision in Electronics:

- **High Precision and Reliability:** Machine vision offers consistency in inspections, reducing errors in production and improving final product reliability.
- **Reduced Scrap and Rework:** Defects are identified early in the production process, minimizing costly scrap and rework.
- **Increased Speed and Throughput:** Automated inspection is faster than manual inspection, keeping up with high-speed production lines in electronics manufacturing.
- **Data Collection for Quality Control:** Vision systems collect data on defect trends, allowing for continuous process improvement and predictive maintenance.

The complexity of electronics manufacturing, combined with the need for precision and reliability, makes machine vision an indispensable tool in this industry.

# Machine vision applications in printing

Machine vision is widely used in the printing industry to ensure high quality, accuracy, and consistency across a variety of printing processes. Here's a look at how machine vision enhances different aspects of printing:

## 1. Print Quality Inspection

- Machine vision systems inspect printed materials to detect print quality issues like smudging, blurring, misalignment, and color inconsistency. This ensures that the output matches the intended design, preserving brand quality and customer satisfaction.

## 2. Color Accuracy and Consistency

- Accurate color reproduction is critical in printing, especially for brand materials and packaging. Machine vision checks for precise color matching, ensuring that colors are consistent across different batches. Vision systems can also monitor color density to maintain uniformity across large print runs.

## 3. Registration and Alignment Verification

- Registration marks are used to ensure different layers of ink or print are correctly aligned. Machine vision verifies these marks, preventing issues like misregistration, where colors or layers don't line up correctly. This is essential for multi-color prints, labels, and packaging.

## 4. Label and Barcode Verification

- For labels and packaging, machine vision checks that barcodes, QR codes, and alphanumeric codes are printed clearly and accurately. It ensures that codes are scannable and comply with regulatory standards, critical for product tracking and inventory management.

## 5. Surface and Substrate Inspection

- Machine vision systems inspect the printing surface, such as paper, plastic, or cardboard, for defects like scratches, dirt, or inconsistencies before printing begins. By verifying substrate quality, it prevents costly errors and reduces waste in the printing process.

## 6. Text and Graphic Positioning

- Vision systems verify that text, logos, and other graphic elements are correctly positioned. They can detect issues like off-center printing or skewed elements and flag them in real time, enabling immediate corrections and reducing the risk of delivering defective prints.

## 7. Printing on Variable Surfaces

- In packaging and label printing, surfaces can vary in texture, shape, and size. Machine vision adapts to these variations, ensuring accurate printing on irregular surfaces. For example, in direct-to-object printing, it ensures print quality even on curved or uneven items.

## 8. Defect Detection in Printed Packaging

- Packaging defects, such as damaged edges, folds, or poor adhesive applications, can affect product appearance and shelf life. Machine vision inspects for such defects, especially in folding cartons, labels, and shrink sleeves, to maintain packaging integrity and presentation quality.

## 9. Pattern and Texture Matching

- Machine vision systems detect and match intricate patterns and textures in printed materials, useful in industries like textiles, wallpaper, and decorative products. It ensures that patterns align correctly and that there are no visual defects, maintaining consistency across large surfaces.

## 10. Security Printing

- Machine vision is essential in security printing applications, like currency, stamps, and high-value documents, to detect unauthorized modifications or forgeries. It inspects for unique security features, such as holograms, micro-text, and UV markings, ensuring authenticity.

## 11. Optical Character Recognition (OCR) and Verification

- OCR is used in the printing industry to read and verify text for traceability or regulatory compliance. It ensures that batch numbers, dates, and other text elements are accurately printed and legible, important in sectors like food and pharmaceuticals.

## 12. Real-time Feedback and Process Control

- Machine vision provides real-time feedback to printing machines, allowing for automated adjustments to print speed, ink density, and alignment. This adaptive control reduces waste and enhances production efficiency by maintaining optimal print quality throughout the process.

## Benefits of Machine Vision in Printing:

- **Consistency and Reliability:** Ensures consistent quality across large print runs, essential for maintaining brand image and product quality.
- **Reduced Waste and Rework:** Detects issues early in the process, minimizing waste and reducing costly reprints.
- **Higher Speed and Efficiency:** Automated inspection allows for high-speed, non-stop production, boosting throughput without compromising quality.
- **Data Collection for Quality Improvement:** Provides data on defects and process trends, enabling continuous improvement and troubleshooting in printing workflows.

With the increasing demand for high-quality printed materials and packaging, machine vision has become a critical tool in the printing industry, helping maintain quality, reduce costs, and ensure compliance with regulatory standards.

# Machine vision applications in pharmaceutical

Machine vision is essential in the pharmaceutical industry, where strict quality, safety, and regulatory standards are critical. By automating inspection and control processes, machine vision enhances accuracy, efficiency, and compliance across production lines. Here are key applications of machine vision in pharmaceuticals:

### 1. Label Verification and Text Inspection

- Machine vision systems verify the accuracy of labels on pharmaceutical packaging, checking for correct placement, legibility, and adherence to regulatory requirements. It ensures information like drug names, dosages, batch numbers, and expiration dates are accurate and readable, reducing the risk of labeling errors.

### 2. Package Integrity and Seal Inspection

- Packaging plays a vital role in protecting pharmaceutical products. Machine vision inspects packaging integrity, including seals, blister packs, bottles, and caps, to prevent contamination or leaks. It ensures packaging is intact and correctly sealed, maintaining product safety and quality.

### 3. Tablet and Capsule Inspection

- Machine vision systems inspect tablets and capsules for defects like cracks, chips, discoloration, or size inconsistencies. They check each tablet or capsule to ensure uniformity in shape, size, and color, as well as verify the presence of each unit in blister packs, helping maintain dosing accuracy.

### 4. Vial and Ampoule Inspection

- Vials and ampoules used for liquid pharmaceuticals require strict inspection. Machine vision examines these containers for defects, such as cracks, scratches, particulates, or fill levels, ensuring that vials and ampoules are safe and meet regulatory requirements.

### 5. Code and Barcode Verification

- Pharmaceuticals require traceability throughout their lifecycle, which includes tracking barcodes, QR codes, and data matrix codes. Machine vision verifies these codes to ensure they are printed accurately and are easily readable, facilitating supply chain tracking and compliance with anti-counterfeiting regulations.

### 6. Optical Character Recognition (OCR) for Text Verification

- OCR technology enables machine vision systems to read and verify printed text, such as batch numbers, expiration dates, and dosage instructions. This ensures that all required information is printed accurately, essential for regulatory compliance and patient safety.

### 7. Bottle and Cap Alignment Verification

- In liquid medicine production, machine vision ensures correct alignment of bottles, caps, and labels. It checks for proper sealing of caps, the presence of tamper-evident seals, and correct label orientation, minimizing contamination risks and ensuring product integrity.

## 8. Blister Pack Inspection

- For blister-packed products, machine vision checks for missing or damaged tablets, proper alignment, and seal integrity. It verifies that each blister cavity contains the correct product and is free of contaminants, ensuring accurate dosing and patient safety.

## 9. Anti-Counterfeiting and Authentication

- Machine vision systems detect security features on pharmaceutical packaging, such as holograms, watermarks, and micro-text, to prevent counterfeiting. This application helps manufacturers and consumers verify the authenticity of products, combating counterfeit drugs in the supply chain.

## 10. Automated Measurement and Dosage Verification

- Machine vision enables precise measurement and dosage verification in the manufacturing of pharmaceuticals. For example, it ensures the correct volume in liquid vials, checks the weight and dimensions of tablets, and verifies consistency in solid dosages, maintaining strict quality standards.

## 11. Defect Detection in Primary and Secondary Packaging

- Primary packaging, like bottles and blister packs, and secondary packaging, like boxes and cartons, are inspected for defects such as dents, creases, or damaged edges. Machine vision ensures that both packaging types are free from defects, protecting the product from damage and contamination.

## 12. Track and Trace for Compliance

- Machine vision supports serialization and track-and-trace systems required for regulatory compliance, particularly with the Drug Supply Chain Security Act (DSCSA) in the U.S. and similar global regulations. It helps track each product unit from production to end consumer, enabling efficient recalls and preventing counterfeit products.

### Benefits of Machine Vision in Pharmaceuticals:

- **Improved Product Quality and Safety:** Machine vision helps maintain the highest standards in product quality and safety, essential in pharmaceuticals where any deviation can have significant health consequences.
- **Reduced Human Error and Increased Precision:** Automated inspection removes human error, providing precise and consistent inspection results.
- **Regulatory Compliance:** Machine vision ensures compliance with stringent pharmaceutical regulations, reducing the risk of non-compliance and associated penalties.
- **Increased Efficiency and Reduced Waste:** Real-time defect detection reduces wastage by identifying errors early in the production process, saving costs and materials.

- **Enhanced Traceability:** By facilitating serialization and traceability, machine vision aids in managing recalls and reducing counterfeit drugs.

With increasing regulatory demands and the need for flawless production, machine vision is integral to pharmaceutical manufacturing, improving quality control, ensuring safety, and boosting efficiency across the supply chain.

# Machine vision applications in textile

Machine vision technology is widely utilized in the textile industry to enhance quality, speed, and efficiency across various stages of production. It helps monitor, inspect, and ensure that textiles meet quality standards, optimizing processes and reducing waste. Here are some key machine vision applications in the textile industry:

## 1. Fabric Defect Detection

- Machine vision systems inspect fabrics in real-time for defects such as tears, holes, stains, color inconsistencies, and pattern mismatches. These systems identify and classify defects, helping manufacturers reduce defective products and maintain quality standards.

## 2. Color Matching and Consistency

- Color consistency is essential in textile production, especially in fabrics used for fashion and home décor. Machine vision systems monitor color during dyeing and printing to ensure each batch matches the specified color exactly. It helps maintain brand quality and reduces the risk of color mismatches across fabric rolls or batches.

## 3. Pattern and Print Inspection

- For patterned fabrics, machine vision verifies that the design is consistent and accurately aligned. This is particularly useful in the production of textiles with intricate patterns or designs, such as plaids, stripes, florals, or custom prints. It detects misaligned or distorted patterns early in the production process.

## 4. Surface Texture Analysis

- Surface texture is a critical quality attribute for many textiles, especially for fabrics with unique textures or finishes. Machine vision analyzes the texture to detect inconsistencies, unwanted knots, or other surface flaws, ensuring that the fabric's tactile qualities meet desired standards.

## 5. Yarn Quality Inspection

- Machine vision systems inspect yarns for consistency, detecting flaws such as uneven thickness, knots, broken fibers, or foreign materials. This helps ensure that only high-quality yarn is used in weaving or knitting, leading to more uniform and durable fabrics.

## 6. Thread and Seam Inspection

- In garment manufacturing, machine vision checks the quality of stitches and seams to identify issues like skipped stitches, loose threads, or misaligned seams. It ensures garment durability and quality while reducing the risk of defects reaching consumers.

## 7. Roll and Batch Inspection

- Machine vision inspects rolls of fabric to ensure that each roll meets the same quality standards without color or pattern discrepancies. This application helps maintain consistency across large batches, crucial in mass production where even minor variations can impact quality.

## 8. Dimension and Size Verification

- Machine vision verifies the dimensions of cut pieces of fabric, ensuring that each piece matches size specifications. It helps in cutting processes, reducing material waste and ensuring that fabric pieces meet exact size requirements for the next stages of production, like stitching or weaving.

## 9. Non-contact Thickness Measurement

- Certain textiles, like carpets or upholstery fabrics, require consistent thickness. Machine vision systems can measure fabric thickness without contact, ensuring uniformity throughout the production process and maintaining product specifications.

## 10. Label and Barcode Verification

- Machine vision checks labels and barcodes printed on textile products for readability and accuracy. This is critical for traceability and inventory management, ensuring that each item is properly tagged and tracked throughout the supply chain.

## 11. 3D Inspection for Upholstery and Furniture Textiles

- Machine vision is used in 3D inspection of textiles designed for upholstery and automotive interiors. It examines the fabric's structure and finish, ensuring it meets both visual and functional standards for applications requiring durability and aesthetic appeal.

## 12. Quality Control in Finishing Processes

- After weaving or knitting, textiles often undergo finishing processes like dyeing, washing, and coating. Machine vision inspects textiles at this stage to detect any irregularities, such as uneven dye application, chemical spots, or fading, ensuring that the finished product is of high quality.

## Benefits of Machine Vision in the Textile Industry:

- **Enhanced Quality Control:** Machine vision systems catch defects early, leading to higher-quality end products and reduced returns or complaints.
- **Increased Production Efficiency:** Automated inspection speeds up the production process, allowing for real-time quality checks without slowing down operations.
- **Reduced Waste and Cost Savings:** By detecting defects early, machine vision helps prevent waste and saves on material costs, leading to more efficient production.
- **Consistency Across Batches:** Machine vision ensures that each roll, batch, or piece of fabric meets the same quality standards, especially important for products requiring uniform appearance and quality.
- **Improved Traceability and Compliance:** Vision systems enable accurate labeling and barcoding, enhancing product traceability and meeting industry standards.

Machine vision is transforming the textile industry by streamlining inspection processes, enhancing quality, and providing valuable insights into production trends, helping manufacturers maintain high standards and meet customer expectations efficiently.

# Machine Vision applications in non-visible spectrum

Machine vision applications in the non-visible spectrum—such as ultraviolet (UV), infrared (IR), and X-ray—enable inspection, analysis, and detection beyond the capabilities of visible light. These non-visible wavelengths are valuable for industries needing specialized inspection techniques to analyze materials, detect flaws, and ensure quality. Here are some key applications of machine vision in the non-visible spectrum:

### 1. Infrared (IR) Vision for Thermal Inspection

- **Thermal Imaging and Temperature Monitoring:** IR machine vision detects and measures temperature changes, useful in applications such as electronics, automotive, and aerospace. For instance, it identifies overheating components, aiding in predictive maintenance and preventing failures.
- **Leak Detection in Sealed Containers:** IR can detect temperature differences caused by leaks in sealed containers, widely used in food and pharmaceutical packaging to ensure product safety and longevity.
- **Quality Control in Welding and Metal Fabrication:** In metal fabrication, IR vision systems inspect welding seams and metal joints by analyzing temperature patterns to detect incomplete welds or structural weaknesses.

### 2. Ultraviolet (UV) Vision for Surface Inspection and Security

- **Surface Contaminant Detection:** UV vision can reveal surface contaminants, such as oils, residues, or chemicals, invisible to visible light. This is important in industries like electronics, pharmaceuticals, and automotive, where clean surfaces are essential for product quality and function.
- **Fluorescent Dye Penetrant Testing:** UV vision systems are used with fluorescent dyes to detect cracks or flaws in materials. The dye penetrates cracks and, under UV light, highlights them, commonly used in non-destructive testing (NDT) for aerospace, automotive, and manufacturing industries.
- **Security and Anti-Counterfeiting:** UV vision verifies security features such as holograms, UV ink, and watermarks on products like currency, passports, and high-value documents. It helps authenticate items and prevent counterfeiting by revealing unique markers only visible under UV light.

### 3. X-ray Vision for Structural and Internal Inspection

- **Internal Defect Detection:** X-ray machine vision is used to inspect internal structures of materials and components, identifying cracks, voids, or inclusions. This is especially important in industries like aerospace and automotive, where structural integrity is critical.
- **Foreign Object Detection in Food and Pharmaceutical Products:** X-ray vision can detect foreign particles or contaminants within packaged products, such as metals or glass in food and pharmaceuticals, ensuring safety and compliance with health regulations.
- **Inspection of Complex Assemblies:** In electronics manufacturing, X-ray vision inspects solder joints and internal connections in printed circuit boards (PCBs) and semiconductor components, essential for high-quality and reliable electronics.

### 4. Shortwave Infrared (SWIR) Vision for Material and Chemical Analysis

- **Moisture and Water Content Detection:** SWIR vision can detect moisture levels in materials, used in industries like food processing and agriculture, where monitoring moisture content is critical for product quality and shelf life.
- **Material Sorting and Recycling:** SWIR can differentiate materials based on their chemical composition, such as distinguishing between different types of plastics or separating organic from inorganic materials. This is valuable in recycling and waste management to enhance sorting efficiency.
- **Quality Control in Pharmaceuticals:** SWIR vision helps verify the uniformity and composition of pharmaceutical products, detecting differences in chemical makeup and ensuring consistency in products like tablets or capsules.

## 5. Hyperspectral Imaging for Composition Analysis and Sorting

- **Agricultural Product Sorting and Quality Control:** Hyperspectral imaging analyzes a wide range of wavelengths to assess the freshness, ripeness, or quality of fruits, vegetables, and grains. It can detect bruises, ripeness, or spoilage beyond what is visible to the naked eye, increasing efficiency in food processing.
- **Pharmaceutical Composition Verification:** Hyperspectral imaging ensures the chemical composition of pharmaceuticals, identifying discrepancies or contamination and helping maintain quality standards.
- **Mining and Mineral Sorting:** Hyperspectral imaging identifies minerals based on their spectral signatures, allowing for precise sorting and grading in the mining industry.

## 6. Terahertz Imaging for Subsurface Inspection

- **Inspection of Non-metallic and Organic Materials:** Terahertz imaging can penetrate non-metallic materials like ceramics, plastics, and composites, making it useful in industries like aerospace, where subsurface defects in composite materials can compromise safety.
- **Detection of Hidden Defects in Coatings and Laminates:** Terahertz vision detects voids, delaminations, and cracks within coatings and laminates, commonly used in quality control for layered materials and coated products.
- **Detection of Foreign Substances in Packaging:** Terahertz vision detects foreign substances in multi-layered packaging, especially in pharmaceuticals and food, where contaminants can compromise product safety.

## Benefits of Non-Visible Spectrum Machine Vision:

- **Enhanced Inspection Capabilities:** Allows detection of features, defects, and contaminants not visible in the standard spectrum, improving quality control in complex materials and processes.
- **Non-Destructive Testing:** Many non-visible spectrum applications allow for non-invasive, non-destructive testing, preserving the integrity of the product while inspecting it for quality.
- **Increased Safety and Compliance:** Non-visible spectrum machine vision enhances safety by identifying potential issues, ensuring compliance with health, safety, and industry-specific standards.
- **Precision and Efficiency:** By detecting issues invisible to visible light, these technologies ensure more accurate inspection, reducing errors and waste in manufacturing.

Applications of machine vision in the non-visible spectrum are expanding across industries, providing insights and quality control measures that help maintain high standards, safety, and compliance in diverse manufacturing processes.

# Machine Vision applications in metrology and gauging

Machine vision plays a critical role in metrology and gauging, providing accurate, non-contact measurement and inspection capabilities that enhance precision, efficiency, and quality in various manufacturing and industrial processes. Here are some key applications of machine vision in metrology and gauging:

## 1. Dimensional Measurement

- Machine vision systems precisely measure dimensions of objects, including length, width, height, diameter, and angles. This application is crucial in industries such as automotive, aerospace, and electronics, where exact dimensions are necessary for component interoperability and quality control.

## 2. Part Alignment and Positioning Verification

- Vision systems verify that parts are aligned and positioned correctly on the production line. This is especially useful in automated assembly processes, ensuring that components are in the proper position before further processing, welding, or assembly.

## 3. Surface Flatness and Profile Inspection

- Machine vision systems inspect the flatness and profile of surfaces to ensure they meet design specifications. This application is vital in precision manufacturing and industries such as aerospace, automotive, and electronics, where surface imperfections can impact performance and safety.

## 4. 3D Measurement and Surface Mapping

- Using stereo vision or laser triangulation, machine vision systems generate 3D models of objects, enabling measurement of complex shapes and contours. This is valuable for inspecting parts with intricate geometries, such as turbine blades or medical devices, ensuring they meet precise specifications.

## 5. Thread and Gear Measurement

- Machine vision inspects threads and gears, measuring parameters like pitch, lead, and depth for threaded parts and checking gear dimensions, tooth shape, and spacing. This ensures proper functionality in mechanical components and assemblies.

## 6. Thickness and Depth Measurement

- Non-contact machine vision systems measure the thickness and depth of materials, such as metals, glass, and plastics. This application is essential in manufacturing processes like metal stamping, glass production, and plastic molding, where material thickness consistency is critical.

## 7. Edge Detection and Chamfer Measurement

- Machine vision systems detect edges and measure chamfers on parts, verifying that each component has the correct edge finish. Edge detection is particularly useful in machining and metalworking, ensuring components fit precisely and maintain durability in assembly.

### 8. Hole and Slot Inspection

- Vision systems measure the diameter, depth, and position of holes and slots, ensuring they are within specified tolerances. This is commonly used in automotive and aerospace manufacturing, where holes must align precisely for components like bolts and rivets.

### 9. Roundness and Cylindricity Measurement

- For cylindrical parts, machine vision checks roundness and cylindricity, ensuring they meet tolerance specifications. This application is important in industries such as automotive and oil & gas, where even slight deviations in roundness can impact functionality and safety.

### 10. Gap and Flush Measurement

- Machine vision inspects gaps and flushness between parts, such as panels or doors in automotive assembly. Ensuring that gaps are consistent and within tolerance improves both aesthetic appeal and functionality, reducing noise, vibration, and potential wear.

### 11. Assembly Verification and Part Counting

- Vision systems verify assembly completeness by counting parts or components, checking for missing, misaligned, or extra components. This is especially useful in high-speed production lines, reducing assembly errors and improving product consistency.

### 12. Weld Seam Inspection

- Machine vision inspects weld seams for continuity, shape, and defects, such as cracks, porosity, or uneven surfaces. This application ensures the structural integrity of welded components in industries like automotive, aerospace, and heavy machinery.

### 13. Automated Caliper Measurement

- Machine vision systems mimic the function of traditional calipers, measuring internal and external dimensions of objects with high accuracy. This enables automated, non-contact measurements for a wide range of objects, streamlining inspection processes and reducing handling time.

### 14. Inline Measurement and Process Control

- Vision systems perform real-time measurements on production lines, providing immediate feedback for process control. By monitoring parts continuously, machine vision detects deviations and helps maintain consistent quality, reducing scrap rates and increasing efficiency.

### 15. Optical Comparator Replacement

- Machine vision systems serve as modern optical comparators, comparing manufactured parts against digital CAD models or reference images. This application automates visual comparison, increasing inspection speed and eliminating human error in critical dimensions and shapes.

**Benefits of Machine Vision in Metrology and Gauging:**

- **High Accuracy and Precision:** Machine vision offers consistent and precise measurements, reducing errors and variability compared to manual methods.
- **Increased Speed and Efficiency:** Automated measurement allows for high-speed inspection, enhancing throughput without compromising accuracy.
- **Non-contact Measurement:** Machine vision measures without touching the object, eliminating wear and tear on sensitive parts and enabling measurement of delicate or moving objects.
- **Real-time Feedback and Process Control:** Inline measurement provides real-time feedback, allowing for immediate adjustments to maintain quality and reduce waste.
- **Improved Quality and Compliance:** Machine vision helps ensure parts meet strict tolerances and regulatory standards, essential in industries like aerospace, automotive, and medical devices.

Machine vision has become indispensable in metrology and gauging, enabling manufacturers to achieve high levels of precision and quality control across a range of applications. This technology not only increases accuracy and efficiency but also contributes to continuous quality improvement in complex manufacturing processes.

# Machine Vision Applications in OCR and OCV

Machine vision applications in Optical Character Recognition (OCR) and Optical Character Verification (OCV) are widely used across industries to automate text recognition and verification processes, enhancing accuracy, traceability, and compliance. Here's an overview of how OCR and OCV are applied:

## 1. Product Identification and Traceability

- OCR enables automated reading of alphanumeric characters on products, such as serial numbers, batch numbers, and expiration dates, crucial for product traceability. This ensures each product can be tracked through its production lifecycle, meeting regulatory standards and aiding in recalls if necessary.
- OCV verifies that printed or marked information, like serial numbers or batch codes, is accurate and complete, ensuring that each product is correctly labeled and traceable.

## 2. Labeling and Packaging Verification

- OCR reads and logs information on packaging, such as product names, ingredients, and other regulatory information, ensuring compliance with industry and safety standards. This is particularly critical in industries like pharmaceuticals and food & beverage, where accurate labeling is essential.
- OCV checks that all label information is correct and matches specified standards. It confirms that labels contain the correct text, reducing the risk of mislabeled products reaching consumers.

## 3. Expiry Date and Lot Code Validation

- OCR reads expiration dates and lot codes on products to ensure information is accurate and legible. This is essential in industries where product shelf life is critical, such as pharmaceuticals, cosmetics, and food & beverage.
- OCV verifies that printed expiration dates and lot codes match the expected format and content. This reduces the risk of expired or misidentified products being distributed, improving safety and compliance.

## 4. Document Processing and Automation

- OCR is used to digitize printed documents, such as invoices, shipping labels, and receipts. This application speeds up data entry, reduces human error, and facilitates document management by automatically extracting and organizing text data.
- OCV is used in document processing to verify that essential information, such as addresses, product names, or quantities, is printed and formatted correctly. This ensures documents are complete and accurate before proceeding in automated workflows.

## 5. Barcode and QR Code Reading and Verification

- OCR reads alphanumeric information associated with barcodes and QR codes, allowing for tracking and data logging. This is essential for inventory management, warehousing, and logistics, where products need to be accurately identified and tracked.
- OCV verifies that codes match the expected data, checking for errors in printing or damaged codes that could impede scanning, thus maintaining efficient and accurate supply chain processes.

## 6. Assembly Verification in Manufacturing

- OCR reads component or part numbers during the assembly process to ensure that the correct parts are being used. This reduces assembly errors and ensures that each product contains the specified components.
- OCV checks that parts are accurately labeled, which is important in industries like automotive and electronics manufacturing, where using the correct part can be crucial for product safety and functionality.

## 7. Document and ID Verification in Security and Access Control

- OCR reads and extracts information from documents like passports, driver's licenses, and ID cards. This application automates the entry of personal information, speeding up processes like airport check-ins and access control.
- OCV verifies that document data, such as names and ID numbers, is accurately printed and formatted. This helps prevent document forgery and ensures data consistency for security purposes.

## 8. Banking and Financial Document Processing

- OCR extracts information from checks, bank statements, and other financial documents, automating data entry and reducing manual effort. This is widely used in banking and financial services for faster processing and document management.
- OCV checks that essential fields, such as account numbers or transaction amounts, are accurately recorded and complete, helping to ensure accuracy and reduce errors in financial transactions.

## 9. Automotive VIN Reading and Verification

- OCR reads Vehicle Identification Numbers (VINs) on cars and auto parts, enabling tracking and identification throughout the vehicle's lifecycle. This is useful for recalls, registrations, and compliance with safety regulations.
- OCV verifies that VINs are printed or engraved correctly, reducing errors in vehicle identification and ensuring accurate data entry for records.

## 10. Pharmaceutical Compliance and Safety

- OCR reads critical text on pharmaceutical packaging, such as dosage instructions, patient information, and regulatory markings. This aids in automated dispensing, packaging, and regulatory compliance.
- OCV verifies that printed information on pharmaceuticals, such as dosage, lot numbers, and patient instructions, meets regulatory standards. This helps prevent labeling errors and ensures patient safety.

## Benefits of OCR and OCV in Machine Vision:

- **Enhanced Traceability and Compliance:** Automating the reading and verification of text ensures accurate tracking of products, meeting regulatory requirements across industries.
- **Reduced Human Error:** Automated text recognition reduces human error in data entry, ensuring accuracy in manufacturing, logistics, and other data-intensive processes.

- **Increased Speed and Efficiency:** OCR and OCV speed up data extraction and verification processes, improving workflow efficiency and reducing bottlenecks.
- **Improved Quality Control:** OCV applications verify that all printed information is correct, consistent, and legible, enhancing quality control and ensuring brand consistency.

Machine vision applications in OCR and OCV are essential for automating and improving data accuracy in text recognition and verification. These technologies play a critical role in quality control, traceability, and regulatory compliance across various industries, from manufacturing to logistics and healthcare.

# Machine Vision applications in vision guided robotics

Machine vision is integral to vision-guided robotics, enabling robots to "see" and respond to their environment. This capability enhances robot flexibility, accuracy, and intelligence in performing a wide range of tasks. Here are some key applications of machine vision in vision-guided robotics:

## 1. Pick and Place Operations

- Vision-guided robots use machine vision to locate, identify, and pick up objects, regardless of their orientation. This is crucial in industries like logistics, electronics, and automotive manufacturing, where parts or packages are often randomly oriented. Vision enables the robot to pick up items precisely and place them in specific locations.

## 2. Object Sorting and Classification

- Machine vision enables robots to sort and classify objects based on size, color, shape, or other visual characteristics. This is especially useful in applications like recycling, food processing, and pharmaceuticals, where robots can sort items into designated categories quickly and accurately.

## 3. Assembly Line and Part Alignment

- Vision-guided robots in assembly lines can recognize parts, align them correctly, and assemble them with high precision. This is commonly seen in automotive and electronics manufacturing, where robots use vision to detect and correctly position parts, ensuring accuracy in complex assemblies.

## 4. Quality Inspection and Defect Detection

- Machine vision-equipped robots inspect products for defects or irregularities in real time. This includes checking for surface defects, measuring dimensions, and ensuring components are correctly assembled. This application improves quality control and reduces the risk of defective products reaching consumers.

## 5. Bin Picking

- Bin picking is a complex task where robots retrieve randomly oriented items from a bin. Vision-guided robots use 3D vision or depth-sensing cameras to locate and grasp items within bins, improving efficiency in tasks like kitting, order fulfillment, and assembly.

## 6. Welding and Seam Tracking

- Vision-guided robots in welding applications use machine vision to follow seams accurately, ensuring precise welds and reducing errors. This application is commonly used in automotive and aerospace industries, where high-quality welds are essential for safety and performance.

## 7. Palletizing and Depalletizing

- Vision-guided robots can identify, stack, and unstack items on pallets, making them efficient for warehouse management, logistics, and e-commerce. Vision allows the robot to identify varying pallet configurations and safely handle items without damage.

## 8. Packaging and Labeling Verification

- Robots equipped with machine vision verify that products are correctly labeled and packaged, inspecting for label position, orientation, and accuracy. This application is critical in industries like food and pharmaceuticals, where correct labeling is essential for compliance and customer safety.

## 9. Autonomous Mobile Robots (AMRs) for Navigation

- Vision-guided AMRs use machine vision for navigation, obstacle detection, and path planning, enabling them to move autonomously in dynamic environments. This is valuable in warehouses and factories, where AMRs transport materials, interact with other machinery, and avoid obstacles.

## 10. Precision Drilling and Machining

- In applications requiring high precision, such as aerospace or electronics manufacturing, vision-guided robots use machine vision to align tools and components precisely for drilling, machining, or assembly. This increases accuracy, reduces errors, and improves production quality.

## 11. Material Handling in Hazardous Environments

- Vision-guided robots are deployed in hazardous or extreme environments, such as nuclear facilities, oil rigs, and chemical plants. Equipped with vision systems, they perform tasks like inspection, maintenance, and material handling in areas dangerous for human workers.

## 12. Painting and Coating

- Vision-guided robots in painting applications use machine vision to detect the shape and orientation of objects, ensuring that paint or coating is applied evenly. This is commonly used in automotive and manufacturing, where uniform coverage is essential for aesthetics and corrosion protection.

## 13. Automated Optical Inspection (AOI) in Electronics

- Vision-guided robots in electronics manufacturing perform AOI, inspecting circuit boards and electronic components for defects. Machine vision detects issues like soldering errors, misaligned components, and missing parts, ensuring high-quality electronic assemblies.

## 14. Human-Robot Collaboration and Safety

- Vision-guided robots monitor human workers in collaborative work environments, detecting proximity and adjusting movements to ensure safety. Machine vision enables robots to work alongside humans safely, taking on repetitive tasks while humans focus on more complex processes.

### Benefits of Machine Vision in Vision-Guided Robotics:

- **Increased Flexibility and Adaptability:** Vision-guided robots adapt to changes in part orientation, shape, and size, allowing them to handle various tasks without reprogramming.
- **Higher Precision and Accuracy:** Machine vision improves positioning accuracy, critical in industries where high precision is essential for quality and safety.
- **Real-Time Decision Making:** Vision systems enable robots to respond dynamically to changes in the environment, making adjustments as necessary to complete tasks accurately.
- **Reduced Setup Time and Cost:** Vision-guided robots require minimal fixtures or part alignment, reducing setup time and overall costs, especially in complex assemblies.
- **Improved Quality Control:** Vision systems identify defects or inconsistencies in real time, improving quality control and reducing the risk of defective products reaching customers.

Vision-guided robotics is a rapidly expanding field, with applications across various industries. By combining machine vision with robotics, manufacturers achieve greater flexibility, precision, and efficiency, transforming traditional manufacturing and production processes into highly automated, adaptive, and intelligent systems.

# Machine Vision in Field and Service Applications

Machine vision technology in field and service applications offers powerful capabilities for inspection, maintenance, monitoring, and data collection outside traditional manufacturing environments. By enabling automated visual analysis and decision-making in the field, machine vision supports various industries, from utilities and infrastructure to agriculture and healthcare. Here are some key applications:

### 1. Infrastructure and Utility Inspection

- **Power Line and Pipeline Inspection:** Machine vision systems, often mounted on drones or robotic arms, inspect power lines, pipelines, and other critical infrastructure for damage, corrosion, or vegetation encroachment. This reduces the need for manual inspections and improves safety, as these tasks are often performed in hard-to-reach or hazardous locations.
- **Bridge and Roadway Monitoring:** Vision systems identify cracks, rust, and structural wear in bridges, tunnels, and roads. By detecting issues early, machine vision contributes to preventive maintenance and prolongs infrastructure lifespan, helping to ensure public safety.

### 2. Agricultural Monitoring and Crop Management

- **Crop Health Monitoring:** Machine vision mounted on drones or ground robots analyzes crop health by assessing color, leaf structure, and texture. Using techniques like multispectral imaging, it detects signs of disease, pests, or nutrient deficiencies, allowing for targeted interventions and more efficient crop management.
- **Fruit and Vegetable Sorting and Harvesting:** Machine vision systems in automated harvesters identify ripe fruits and vegetables based on color, size, and texture. It helps improve harvest quality and efficiency, reducing labor costs and minimizing waste.

### 3. Forestry and Environmental Monitoring

- **Tree Health and Growth Assessment:** Vision systems analyze trees in forests, assessing growth rates, health, and potential threats like pest infestations. This data aids in sustainable forestry management and conservation efforts.
- **Wildlife and Habitat Monitoring:** Machine vision identifies and tracks wildlife and changes in habitats, which is valuable for ecological research and conservation. For example, it can detect endangered species or monitor the impact of climate change on natural habitats.

### 4. Building and Facility Maintenance

- **Roof and Wall Inspections:** Machine vision detects leaks, cracks, and structural damage in building roofs, walls, and façades. Using drones equipped with thermal or IR cameras, it identifies potential issues like heat loss or water damage, enabling timely repairs and improving building efficiency.
- **HVAC and Electrical System Monitoring:** Vision systems monitor HVAC systems, electrical panels, and machinery, detecting overheating or other signs of wear. This improves facility maintenance by enabling predictive maintenance and reducing the likelihood of equipment failures.

### 5. Oil and Gas Field Inspection

- **Leak Detection and Corrosion Monitoring:** Machine vision, particularly infrared and thermal imaging, detects leaks and corrosion in pipelines, tanks, and valves. These inspections improve safety by identifying risks early, especially in hazardous environments like offshore rigs and refineries.
- **Equipment Condition Monitoring:** Vision systems inspect equipment like pumps, compressors, and drilling machinery for signs of wear and tear, helping to prevent breakdowns and ensuring operational safety in oil and gas fields.

## 6. Mining and Resource Extraction

- **Ore Quality and Grading:** Machine vision is used in mining to analyze ore quality, ensuring the extracted materials meet required specifications. This is done by identifying differences in mineral composition or detecting impurities, enabling more efficient sorting and reducing processing costs.
- **Equipment and Site Safety Monitoring:** Vision systems monitor mining equipment and surroundings, detecting any safety hazards or changes in the environment that could lead to accidents, like rockfalls or machinery failures. This enhances safety in remote and challenging mining environments.

## 7. Healthcare and Medical Field Services

- **Telemedicine and Remote Diagnostics:** Machine vision supports remote diagnostics by analyzing medical images and assisting healthcare professionals in assessing conditions like skin lesions, dental issues, or wound healing. This enables more accessible healthcare in rural or underserved areas.
- **Medical Equipment Monitoring:** Vision systems monitor medical devices, such as infusion pumps and ventilators, for correct operation. Machine vision detects potential malfunctions or incorrect usage, enhancing patient safety and equipment reliability in field hospitals or remote clinics.

## 8. Disaster Response and Search and Rescue

- **Debris and Hazard Identification:** Machine vision-equipped drones or robots analyze debris fields, identify hazardous materials, and locate potential survivors in disaster zones. This application supports faster, safer response efforts by helping first responders navigate dangerous environments.
- **Thermal Imaging for Human Detection:** Thermal imaging combined with machine vision helps locate people trapped in rubble or hard-to-reach areas during search and rescue missions, especially in low visibility or nighttime conditions.

## 9. Transportation and Logistics

- **Vehicle and Cargo Inspection:** Vision systems at border checkpoints, ports, or loading docks inspect vehicles and cargo for security risks, contraband, or hazardous materials. Automated inspections improve safety and speed up processing times in logistics and transportation.
- **Traffic Monitoring and Incident Detection:** Machine vision monitors traffic conditions, detects incidents, and identifies vehicles involved in accidents. This data improves traffic management and assists emergency responders in addressing incidents more efficiently.

## 10. Public Safety and Security

- **Facial Recognition for Access Control:** Machine vision enables facial recognition in access control systems for buildings or sensitive locations, enhancing security by verifying individuals' identities.
- **Crowd Monitoring and Behavior Analysis:** Vision systems analyze crowd movements and detect unusual behavior or potential hazards. This is useful in public spaces, events, and large gatherings to enhance security and safety.

**Benefits of Machine Vision in Field and Service Applications:**

- **Remote Monitoring and Accessibility:** Machine vision enables inspections and monitoring in hard-to-reach or hazardous locations, reducing the need for human presence and improving safety.
- **Early Detection and Predictive Maintenance:** By detecting issues early, machine vision helps prevent costly failures and allows for preventive maintenance, extending the lifespan of assets.
- **Improved Accuracy and Consistency:** Automated visual analysis is consistent and precise, reducing human error and enhancing data reliability in critical applications.
- **Cost Savings and Operational Efficiency:** By streamlining inspection and monitoring processes, machine vision lowers operational costs and enhances productivity, particularly in fieldwork and remote service environments.
- **Enhanced Safety and Compliance:** Machine vision helps meet regulatory requirements and improves safety by detecting hazards, monitoring environmental conditions, and supporting safe operation in challenging settings.

Machine vision in field and service applications is transforming how inspections, maintenance, and monitoring tasks are conducted. By offering real-time, automated insights, machine vision enhances safety, reliability, and efficiency in diverse industries, from utilities to healthcare and environmental management.

# Machine Vision Applications in Agriculture

Machine vision technology has revolutionized agriculture by enabling precise, automated, and data-driven decisions to optimize crop health, yield, and efficiency. Here are some key applications of machine vision in agriculture:

### 1. Crop Health Monitoring

- Machine vision systems, often mounted on drones or autonomous vehicles, analyze plant health by assessing leaf color, shape, and texture. These systems can detect signs of diseases, pests, or nutrient deficiencies early, allowing for targeted intervention and reducing crop loss.
- By using multispectral or hyperspectral imaging, machine vision can assess specific wavelengths to identify plant stress indicators invisible to the naked eye.

### 2. Weed Detection and Removal

- Machine vision differentiates between crops and weeds, enabling targeted weed management. This is commonly used in precision spraying systems that spray herbicide only on detected weeds, reducing chemical usage and minimizing environmental impact.
- Autonomous weed removal robots utilize machine vision to identify and physically remove weeds without harming the surrounding crops, reducing dependency on herbicides and enhancing organic farming practices.

### 3. Yield Estimation and Crop Counting

- Vision systems count fruits, vegetables, or grains on plants to estimate yield. This application helps farmers plan harvests, manage resources, and make data-driven decisions to maximize crop yield and minimize waste.
- By analyzing fruit size and count on trees or vines, machine vision can provide accurate yield predictions, aiding in logistics, storage planning, and market pricing.

### 4. Automated Harvesting

- Machine vision is essential for robotic harvesters, helping them identify ripe fruits or vegetables based on color, size, and shape. Robots equipped with machine vision can harvest crops precisely, reducing damage to produce and minimizing labor costs.
- In crops like strawberries, apples, and tomatoes, vision-guided robots selectively harvest fruits that meet ripeness criteria, reducing waste and improving harvest quality.

### 5. Irrigation Management and Soil Analysis

- Machine vision detects soil moisture levels and assesses plant water needs, allowing for optimized irrigation management. By analyzing color and texture changes in soil or leaves, it helps determine when and where to irrigate, conserving water and improving crop health.
- Some systems integrate with smart irrigation systems to automate water distribution, ensuring crops receive just the right amount of water based on their specific needs.

## 6. Nutrient Deficiency Detection

- Using color analysis, machine vision detects nutrient deficiencies in plants, such as nitrogen, phosphorus, or potassium deficiencies. These deficiencies often manifest as specific color changes in leaves, and early detection allows for timely corrective measures, improving crop yield and health.

## 7. Disease and Pest Detection

- Machine vision can identify disease symptoms on leaves and stems, such as spotting, discoloration, or wilting, providing early alerts for pest or disease management. This allows for targeted pesticide application, reducing chemical use and minimizing environmental impact.
- Drones equipped with vision systems can monitor large fields for pest infestations, enabling faster response times and reducing the spread of pests.

## 8. Fruit and Vegetable Sorting and Grading

- Machine vision systems in processing facilities sort and grade fruits, vegetables, and grains based on size, color, shape, and defects. This application ensures that produce meets quality standards before reaching the market, improving consumer satisfaction and reducing food waste.
- By automating sorting and grading, machine vision also improves efficiency in packaging facilities, handling high volumes with speed and consistency.

## 9. Livestock Monitoring and Health Assessment

- Machine vision monitors livestock for behavior patterns, movement, and physical conditions, helping farmers assess animal health and detect signs of illness or stress. It can analyze feeding patterns, weight gain, and other indicators, contributing to healthier livestock and higher productivity.
- For dairy farms, machine vision systems analyze the physical condition of cattle, assessing aspects like weight, gait, and udder health, aiding in herd management and disease prevention.

## 10. Phenotyping and Plant Breeding

- Machine vision is used in plant phenotyping to assess various traits, such as growth rate, leaf area, and stress response. Researchers use this data to develop new crop varieties with desired traits, such as drought resistance, improved yield, or disease resistance.
- By automating phenotyping, machine vision accelerates the breeding process and enhances precision, allowing researchers to analyze large data sets efficiently.

## 11. Precision Spraying and Fertilization

- Machine vision enables precision spraying of fertilizers, pesticides, or herbicides by targeting specific areas in need. Mounted on drones or autonomous vehicles, these systems identify target areas and spray with high precision, reducing chemical use and minimizing environmental harm.
- This application is particularly valuable in large-scale agriculture, where traditional blanket spraying methods are costly and inefficient.

## 12. Soil Erosion and Field Monitoring

- Machine vision analyzes soil quality and erosion patterns, providing data to optimize field management. This is important for preventing soil degradation, conserving nutrients, and maintaining field health over the long term.
- Drones equipped with machine vision can capture aerial data on field conditions, including topography, water distribution, and erosion, helping farmers make informed decisions about crop placement, soil amendment, and conservation practices.

## Benefits of Machine Vision in Agriculture:

- **Increased Precision and Efficiency:** Machine vision systems improve precision in detecting crop health, managing pests, and optimizing resource use, resulting in healthier crops and higher yields.
- **Reduced Labor Costs and Dependence:** Automation of labor-intensive tasks like harvesting and sorting reduces labor costs, enabling farmers to manage large-scale operations more efficiently.
- **Enhanced Sustainability:** Targeted spraying and irrigation reduce chemical use and water waste, minimizing environmental impact and promoting more sustainable farming practices.
- **Early Detection and Intervention:** Early detection of disease, pests, and nutrient deficiencies allows for timely intervention, reducing crop losses and enhancing productivity.
- **Data-Driven Decisions:** Machine vision provides valuable data insights that allow farmers to make informed decisions, helping optimize inputs, improve yields, and manage crops more effectively.

Machine vision is transforming agriculture into a high-tech industry, allowing for more efficient, sustainable, and productive farming. By integrating with drones, autonomous vehicles, and smart farming technologies, machine vision supports precision agriculture, enabling farmers to monitor, analyze, and manage crops and livestock with unprecedented accuracy and insight.

# Machine Vision Applications in Bio Medical field

Machine vision has a transformative impact on the biomedical field, supporting applications in diagnostics, surgical assistance, laboratory automation, and patient monitoring. Here's a look at the main applications of machine vision in the biomedical field:

## 1. Medical Imaging and Diagnostics

- **Disease Detection and Analysis:** Machine vision systems analyze medical images (e.g., X-rays, MRIs, CT scans, ultrasounds) to detect signs of diseases like tumors, fractures, infections, or abnormalities. Algorithms can automatically detect anomalies, helping radiologists make quicker and more accurate diagnoses.
- **Pathology and Cytology:** Vision systems assist in analyzing cell and tissue samples for pathology and cytology, enabling automated cell counting, detecting irregular cell structures, and identifying malignancies in tissues. This reduces diagnostic time and increases the accuracy of pathology reports.

## 2. Surgical Assistance and Guidance

- **Robot-Assisted Surgery:** Machine vision provides real-time imaging for robotic surgical systems, enhancing precision in minimally invasive surgeries. Vision-guided robotic systems help surgeons visualize anatomical structures, navigate complex tissues, and execute delicate movements accurately.
- **Augmented Reality in Surgery:** Machine vision powers augmented reality systems in surgery, overlaying vital information, such as blood vessels or tumor boundaries, onto the surgical field. This helps surgeons navigate complex procedures with improved precision and patient safety.

## 3. Microscopy and Cellular Analysis

- **Automated Cell Counting:** Machine vision systems in microscopy automatically count cells, quantify cell types, and analyze growth patterns. This is essential in research and clinical labs where counting accuracy is critical for cell culture analysis and drug testing.
- **Subcellular Analysis:** Vision systems analyze cell structures at the subcellular level, such as detecting abnormalities in mitochondria, nuclei, and other organelles. This application aids in studying cellular functions, disease mechanisms, and the effects of various treatments on cells.

## 4. Biomedical Research and Drug Discovery

- **High-Content Screening (HCS):** Machine vision accelerates drug discovery by enabling high-content screening, where thousands of compounds are tested for their biological effects on cells. Vision systems analyze cellular responses to different compounds, identifying promising candidates for further testing.
- **Genomic and Proteomic Analysis:** Machine vision automates image analysis in genomics and proteomics, aiding in the study of DNA, RNA, and protein structures. It enables rapid sequencing, cell tracking, and biomarker detection, contributing to personalized medicine and targeted treatments.

## 5. Blood Analysis and Hematology

- **Automated Blood Cell Classification:** Machine vision systems in hematology classify blood cells, identifying abnormalities like anemia, leukopenia, or other blood disorders. It enables rapid, accurate blood analysis without requiring intensive manual labor.
- **Flow Cytometry:** Machine vision aids in flow cytometry, analyzing cell characteristics in blood or tissue samples. This application supports immunophenotyping, cell sorting, and cancer diagnosis, playing a vital role in disease detection and research.

## 6. Histology and Tissue Analysis

- **Tissue Slide Scanning and Analysis:** Machine vision digitizes and analyzes histological slides, identifying structures, lesions, and abnormalities in tissues. Automated tissue analysis reduces the time pathologists spend examining slides, enhancing diagnostic throughput.
- **Quantification of Biomarkers:** In oncology and other specialties, machine vision quantifies biomarkers in tissue samples, helping in diagnosis and treatment planning. This is critical in identifying tumor types, cancer staging, and assessing treatment response.

## 7. Lab Automation and Sample Analysis

- **Automated Sample Sorting and Tracking:** Machine vision identifies and tracks samples in laboratory automation systems, ensuring each sample is correctly labeled, sorted, and routed. This increases efficiency and reduces errors in high-volume labs.
- **Quality Control in Sample Preparation:** Vision systems verify the quality of prepared samples, such as ensuring proper labeling, correct amounts, and absence of contaminants. This is particularly useful in clinical and research labs where sample integrity is critical.

## 8. Endoscopy and In Vivo Imaging

- **Enhanced Visualization in Endoscopy:** Machine vision enhances endoscopic images, helping doctors visualize internal organs and tissues more clearly. Real-time image processing can highlight features such as lesions or vascular structures, aiding in minimally invasive procedures.
- **Capsule Endoscopy:** In capsule endoscopy, a small, ingestible camera captures images inside the gastrointestinal tract. Machine vision analyzes these images to detect abnormalities like polyps, inflammation, or bleeding, providing a non-invasive diagnostic option.

## 9. Dental Imaging and Orthodontics

- **Tooth and Bone Analysis:** Machine vision assists in dental imaging, detecting cavities, decay, and bone loss. It is used to analyze X-rays, CBCT (Cone Beam Computed Tomography), and other dental images, helping dentists diagnose conditions accurately.
- **Orthodontic Planning:** Machine vision supports orthodontic planning by mapping dental structures, measuring tooth positioning, and simulating treatment outcomes. This enables personalized treatment plans and improves orthodontic outcomes.

## 10. Biometric and Patient Identification

- **Facial Recognition for Patient ID:** Machine vision is used in healthcare settings for secure patient identification, minimizing errors in medical record retrieval and treatment. This is particularly beneficial in large hospitals where manual patient identification is prone to errors.
- **Gait Analysis for Rehabilitation:** In rehabilitation, machine vision monitors patient movement and gait, helping to assess recovery and adjust treatment plans. Gait analysis is essential in physical therapy for injury recovery and patients with movement disorders.

### 11. Telemedicine and Remote Patient Monitoring

- **Vital Sign Monitoring:** Machine vision systems monitor vital signs, such as heart rate, respiratory rate, and oxygen saturation, through remote cameras. This non-contact monitoring supports telemedicine and home healthcare, providing essential data for remote patient management.
- **Wound and Skin Condition Assessment:** Machine vision allows remote monitoring of wound healing, skin conditions, or dermatological issues. It helps healthcare providers assess wound progression, identify infection signs, and offer treatment recommendations remotely.

### 12. Contamination Detection and Sterility Verification

- **Detection of Foreign Objects in Medical Equipment:** Machine vision systems inspect medical equipment and devices for contamination, foreign objects, or assembly errors. This ensures that instruments and devices meet stringent safety standards before use in patient care.
- **Surface Sterility Checks:** In laboratory and surgical environments, machine vision checks surfaces for sterility and cleanliness, identifying contaminants or residue that could compromise patient safety or experimental integrity.

### Benefits of Machine Vision in Biomedical Applications:

- **Enhanced Precision and Accuracy:** Machine vision improves diagnostic accuracy, surgical precision, and laboratory analysis, minimizing human error and enabling more reliable results.
- **Higher Efficiency and Throughput:** Automation in imaging and analysis speeds up processes, allowing healthcare providers and researchers to handle high volumes of data and samples more efficiently.
- **Early Detection and Preventive Care:** Early detection of diseases and abnormalities through machine vision enables timely intervention, improving patient outcomes and potentially reducing treatment costs.
- **Data-Driven Insights:** Machine vision systems provide valuable insights through detailed analysis of medical images and samples, supporting data-driven decisions in diagnostics, research, and treatment.
- **Improved Patient Safety and Compliance:** By ensuring accurate identification, sterility, and quality control, machine vision helps maintain high standards of patient safety and regulatory compliance.

Machine vision in the biomedical field is rapidly advancing, transforming how healthcare and research professionals diagnose, treat, and monitor patients. By enhancing precision, speed, and safety, machine vision contributes to improved outcomes, streamlined workflows, and a more efficient healthcare ecosystem.

# Machine Vision applications in augmented reality

Machine vision plays a crucial role in augmented reality (AR) by enabling precise tracking, recognition, and contextual understanding of the physical environment. These capabilities enhance the interactivity and immersion of AR experiences across various applications. Here are some key applications of machine vision in augmented reality:

### 1. Object Recognition and Tracking

- Machine vision in AR systems can recognize and track physical objects, such as furniture, appliances, or tools, and overlay digital information or guidance onto them. For example, AR apps in retail allow customers to view virtual furniture in their living spaces, aiding in the purchasing decision.
- In industrial applications, machine vision tracks and identifies equipment, enabling maintenance workers to view real-time data or instructional overlays on machinery, improving efficiency and reducing errors.

### 2. Face Recognition and Augmented Interactions

- Machine vision in AR is used for facial recognition, enabling personalized content and interactions. For instance, social media filters and apps use face tracking to overlay digital effects or animations on users' faces, enhancing the interactive experience.
- Facial recognition also allows AR systems to identify individuals in applications like security, access control, and user authentication, ensuring a secure and personalized experience.

### 3. Pose Estimation and Gesture Recognition

- Machine vision enables pose estimation, where AR systems detect human body poses and movements. This capability allows users to interact with virtual content using gestures or body movements, enhancing the interactivity of AR applications in gaming, fitness, and training.
- Gesture recognition in AR is valuable in virtual training and simulation, where users can perform specific actions that the system recognizes and responds to, providing real-time feedback.

### 4. Environment Mapping and SLAM (Simultaneous Localization and Mapping)

- SLAM allows AR systems to map the environment and track the user's position within it, enabling realistic placement and scaling of virtual objects. Machine vision-based SLAM creates an accurate 3D map of the surroundings, crucial for dynamic AR applications where users move through complex spaces.
- This is essential for applications in navigation, gaming, and industrial training, where AR content must stay aligned with the physical environment as users move.

### 5. Image Recognition and Visual Search

- Machine vision allows AR systems to recognize images or objects in the physical world and provide relevant information. For example, users can point their AR device at a product or artwork to receive information about it, such as price, history, or specifications, creating an interactive educational or shopping experience.

- Visual search in AR is useful in retail and tourism, where users can instantly access detailed information by scanning items in stores, museums, or historical sites.

## 6. Indoor Navigation and Wayfinding

- Machine vision enables AR-powered indoor navigation by recognizing landmarks, pathways, or signs within buildings. Users receive directional overlays on their screens, guiding them through complex environments like airports, shopping malls, or hospitals.
- Indoor navigation is especially helpful for visually impaired individuals, providing auditory or visual cues to enhance spatial awareness and mobility in indoor spaces.

## 7. Augmented Reality in Surgery and Medical Visualization

- Machine vision enhances AR in medical applications by overlaying digital data onto a patient's body, helping surgeons visualize anatomy, blood vessels, or tumors during procedures. This improves precision in complex surgeries and minimizes invasiveness.
- AR also aids in diagnostic procedures, enabling doctors to visualize imaging data, such as CT or MRI scans, directly on the patient, facilitating a deeper understanding of conditions and improving patient outcomes.

## 8. Industrial and Equipment Maintenance

- Machine vision-enabled AR assists in industrial maintenance by identifying equipment and overlaying step-by-step instructions or diagnostics. This application is particularly valuable in complex machinery maintenance, where AR guides technicians through repair processes, reducing downtime and increasing efficiency.
- AR-based maintenance applications enhance safety and accuracy by providing real-time visual information on operational parameters, wear levels, and error alerts.

## 9. Training and Simulation

- Machine vision in AR is widely used in training and simulation applications across industries like aerospace, military, and medical fields. AR overlays virtual elements onto real-world equipment, allowing trainees to interact with realistic simulations and gain hands-on experience without risks.
- Machine vision can track users' actions and provide instant feedback, making the training experience interactive, immersive, and tailored to individual learning progress.

## 10. Retail and E-commerce Applications

- In retail, machine vision enables AR applications that allow users to visualize products, such as clothing, makeup, or furniture, in real-time. AR mirrors let customers try on virtual items before purchasing, improving the shopping experience and reducing return rates.
- For e-commerce, machine vision-powered AR apps enable customers to "place" virtual items in their homes, such as viewing how furniture would look in their space, facilitating more informed purchase decisions.

## 11. Architectural Visualization and Real Estate

- AR systems in real estate and architecture use machine vision to visualize buildings, layouts, and room designs. By mapping the physical environment, AR enables clients to see how new structures or renovations would appear in real-world settings.
- Machine vision-powered AR apps allow architects and designers to showcase different design options interactively, enhancing client engagement and decision-making.

## 12. Augmented Reality in Education

- Machine vision applications in AR are transforming education by allowing students to interact with digital content overlaid on real-world objects. For example, students can view 3D models of the human body, molecules, or historical artifacts in AR, providing an engaging and immersive learning experience.
- AR-based learning is particularly beneficial for STEM education, where complex subjects are visualized and explained interactively, increasing comprehension and retention.

## 13. Automotive and Autonomous Vehicle Assistance

- Machine vision in AR is used in automotive applications to overlay navigation data, traffic information, and hazard warnings on windshields or screens. This enhances driver safety and situational awareness, providing real-time information without distracting the driver.
- In autonomous vehicles, AR interfaces give passengers real-time insights into the vehicle's surroundings and route, building trust in the technology by keeping users informed of the car's decisions.

### Benefits of Machine Vision in Augmented Reality:

- **Enhanced Interactivity and User Experience:** Machine vision provides real-time tracking, object recognition, and gesture detection, creating a more interactive and immersive AR experience.
- **Improved Accuracy and Precision:** Machine vision ensures that virtual elements are aligned correctly with the real world, essential for applications like medical imaging, training, and navigation.
- **Increased Efficiency and Productivity:** By overlaying instructions, data, and visuals directly onto equipment or tasks, machine vision-based AR reduces errors and increases productivity in fields like maintenance, logistics, and training.
- **Personalization and Adaptability:** Machine vision in AR enables personalized content, such as face recognition or custom overlays, enhancing the user experience in sectors like retail, gaming, and healthcare.
- **Real-Time Decision Support:** Machine vision-based AR provides instant access to contextual information, enabling users to make quick, informed decisions in dynamic environments.

Machine vision applications in AR are evolving rapidly, bringing advanced capabilities to industries such as healthcare, retail, education, and manufacturing. By merging digital content with the real world in accurate, interactive ways, machine vision enables AR systems to deliver practical, immersive experiences that add significant value across various domains.

# Machine Vision applications in surveillance

Machine vision plays an increasingly important role in surveillance, enhancing capabilities for security, monitoring, and analytics across various environments. Here are some key applications of machine vision in surveillance:

### 1. Facial Recognition

- Machine vision enables facial recognition in surveillance systems, identifying individuals in real time. This application is widely used in access control, airports, and public spaces to detect and verify identities, ensuring security and aiding in criminal identification.
- Advanced machine vision algorithms can also detect specific attributes, such as age, gender, and emotional expressions, providing additional context in surveillance footage for enhanced situational awareness.

### 2. Intrusion Detection and Perimeter Security

- Machine vision detects unauthorized access or intrusion within restricted areas, such as perimeter boundaries, sensitive locations, and military facilities. By recognizing movement patterns and unusual behaviors, it triggers alarms or alerts, allowing security personnel to respond proactively.
- In industrial or critical infrastructure sites, machine vision can monitor large areas continuously, ensuring that perimeter security remains intact even in low-light conditions or adverse weather.

### 3. Object Detection and Tracking

- Surveillance systems use machine vision to detect and track objects, such as vehicles, bags, or equipment, in real time. This is essential for monitoring public spaces, transportation hubs, and critical infrastructure where unattended or suspicious objects pose security risks.
- Object tracking also aids in following persons of interest within crowded areas, enabling security teams to keep tabs on suspects or potential threats more effectively.

### 4. License Plate Recognition (LPR)

- Machine vision-based license plate recognition is used in traffic monitoring, parking management, toll collection, and access control systems. By identifying vehicle plates in real time, LPR enhances road safety, supports law enforcement in tracking vehicles, and facilitates automated vehicle access management.
- LPR systems are also valuable for smart cities and law enforcement agencies, helping monitor traffic flow, identify stolen vehicles, and enforce traffic regulations.

### 5. Crowd Counting and Density Analysis

- In public venues, machine vision estimates crowd density and counts individuals to monitor capacity and ensure safety. This is useful for large gatherings, such as concerts, stadiums, and festivals, where overcrowding could pose safety risks.

- Crowd density analysis can alert authorities when crowding reaches unsafe levels, enabling quick action to manage or disperse crowds, improving overall public safety.

## 6. Behavior Analysis and Anomaly Detection

- Machine vision-based behavioral analysis detects unusual or suspicious activities, such as loitering, running, or aggressive movements. By establishing normal activity patterns, machine vision identifies deviations in behavior that may indicate potential security incidents.
- Anomaly detection is used in banks, airports, and other high-security areas to alert security personnel of possible threats, such as unauthorized access attempts or aggressive behavior.

## 7. Fire and Smoke Detection

- Machine vision systems detect smoke, flames, or unusual heat signatures in real time, providing early alerts for potential fires. This application is crucial in settings such as warehouses, factories, and public buildings, where early fire detection can prevent costly damage and save lives.
- By analyzing smoke and fire patterns, machine vision also distinguishes between real threats and harmless conditions (like fog), reducing false alarms.

## 8. Left-Behind Object Detection

- Surveillance systems equipped with machine vision can detect unattended objects in public spaces, such as airports, train stations, and shopping malls. This is particularly important in identifying potentially hazardous objects or abandoned bags, prompting quick action to ensure public safety.
- Machine vision helps monitor for left-behind objects even in busy environments, alerting security personnel to inspect or remove suspicious items efficiently.

## 9. People Counting and Flow Analysis in Retail and Transportation

- Machine vision systems count people entering and exiting buildings, analyzing foot traffic patterns in retail stores, malls, and transportation hubs. This data helps in managing crowd flow, optimizing staff deployment, and improving facility management.
- In retail, people counting also provides insights into shopper behavior, enabling retailers to enhance customer experience and optimize store layouts based on foot traffic patterns.

## 10. Vehicle Detection and Traffic Monitoring

- Machine vision detects and monitors vehicles in real time, providing insights into traffic flow, congestion, and incidents. This data is critical for urban planning, traffic management, and reducing congestion in busy city centers.
- Real-time traffic monitoring also supports emergency response by identifying accidents or road obstructions, enabling faster response times and improving road safety.

## 11. Biometric Surveillance and Identity Verification

- Besides facial recognition, machine vision-based biometric surveillance includes iris recognition, gait analysis, and voice recognition to identify individuals. These methods enhance security in high-risk areas where multi-factor identity verification is required.
- Biometric surveillance provides accurate, non-intrusive identification, improving access control in facilities like government buildings, banks, and data centers.

### 12. Thermal Imaging for Low-Visibility Environments

- Machine vision in thermal imaging detects heat signatures, allowing surveillance in low-visibility conditions like fog, smoke, or darkness. This is particularly useful for monitoring areas with minimal lighting, such as border patrols, remote industrial sites, and nighttime surveillance.
- Thermal imaging can also help detect intruders or wildlife in sensitive areas like national parks or wildlife reserves, ensuring safety and conservation without requiring visible lighting.

### 13. Intelligent Video Analytics and Forensic Search

- Machine vision enhances video analytics by automatically tagging events, objects, and behaviors in recorded footage, making it easier to search and analyze surveillance data. For instance, security personnel can search for specific objects, people, or vehicles across extensive footage.
- Intelligent video analytics streamline forensic investigations, enabling authorities to quickly find relevant evidence or identify persons of interest after an incident.

### 14. AR-Based Surveillance for Real-Time Information Overlay

- Augmented reality (AR) surveillance overlays real-time information onto surveillance feeds, enhancing situational awareness for security personnel. For example, personnel can view location-specific data, building layouts, or nearby personnel locations in AR, aiding in coordinated responses to incidents.
- AR-based surveillance is particularly valuable in large facilities like airports, stadiums, or factories, where quick access to detailed information is essential for effective incident response.

### 15. Automated Alert Generation and Incident Reporting

- Machine vision systems can automatically generate alerts based on predefined criteria, such as unauthorized access, vehicle speed violations, or suspicious behavior. These alerts notify security personnel in real time, allowing them to respond quickly to potential threats.
- Incident reporting is also streamlined with machine vision, as it can automatically document events with timestamps, locations, and descriptions, providing valuable data for security audits and post-incident analysis.

### Benefits of Machine Vision in Surveillance:

- **Enhanced Security and Safety:** Machine vision systems improve security by detecting threats early, monitoring suspicious behavior, and identifying persons of interest, making public and private spaces safer.
- **Real-Time Monitoring and Response:** Automated detection and alerting enable faster response times in security incidents, ensuring immediate intervention and reducing risks.

- **Cost Savings and Efficiency:** Machine vision reduces the need for constant human monitoring, allowing security personnel to focus on more critical tasks and making surveillance more cost-effective.
- **Data-Driven Insights and Predictive Analysis:** Vision systems collect and analyze vast amounts of data, helping in predictive analysis, trend identification, and making informed decisions for resource allocation.
  - **Reduced Human Error and Fatigue:** Machine vision automates tedious surveillance tasks, reducing reliance on human operators, who may miss critical events due to fatigue or distractions.

Machine vision applications in surveillance enhance the effectiveness of security measures by providing automated, intelligent, and data-driven solutions. From real-time threat detection to detailed forensic analysis, machine vision makes surveillance systems more robust, responsive, and efficient across various sectors, including public safety, transportation, retail, and industrial security.

# Machine Vision applications in bio-metrics

Machine vision plays a critical role in biometric applications by enabling automated, precise, and efficient identification and verification processes across various environments. Biometric systems use unique physical or behavioral characteristics to verify identities, and machine vision provides the capabilities necessary to capture, analyze, and authenticate these biometrics. Here are some key applications of machine vision in biometrics:

## 1. Facial Recognition

- **Identity Verification:** Machine vision detects and analyzes facial features such as the distance between eyes, nose shape, and jawline to create unique faceprints for individual identification. This application is widely used in access control, banking, and security systems to authenticate identities quickly and accurately.
- **Surveillance and Law Enforcement:** Facial recognition technology aids law enforcement by identifying suspects or persons of interest in crowds or public spaces. Real-time facial recognition can detect matches against watchlists, enhancing public safety and supporting criminal investigations.

## 2. Iris Recognition

- Machine vision systems capture high-resolution images of the iris, analyzing its unique patterns, which remain stable throughout a person's life. Iris recognition is widely used in secure environments such as airports, government facilities, and banking, where a high level of security is essential.
- This technology provides an extremely reliable form of authentication because the iris has complex patterns unique to each individual, making it resistant to impersonation or duplication.

## 3. Fingerprint Recognition

- **Identity Authentication:** Machine vision captures detailed fingerprint images, analyzing patterns like ridges, whorls, and minutiae points unique to each fingerprint. This application is widely used in mobile devices, time attendance systems, and law enforcement to verify identities securely and accurately.
- **Forensics:** Fingerprint recognition is crucial in forensic investigations, where machine vision assists in matching fingerprints collected at crime scenes against criminal databases. This helps investigators identify suspects and link individuals to crime scenes.

## 4. Palm Vein Recognition

- Machine vision systems detect vein patterns under the skin of the palm, using near-infrared imaging to capture unique vein structures. This biometric method is highly secure and difficult to forge, commonly used in banking and healthcare for identity verification.
- Palm vein recognition is preferred in some applications because vein patterns are invisible to the naked eye, making them difficult to counterfeit and ensuring a high level of security.

## 5. Gait Analysis

- Machine vision captures and analyzes a person's gait, which is the unique way they walk. Gait analysis is useful for unobtrusive identification in public spaces, such as airports or high-security facilities, where traditional biometrics like fingerprints may not be feasible.
- Gait recognition is also beneficial in identifying individuals from a distance, and it remains effective even if facial features are obscured, making it valuable for covert surveillance and security.

## 6. Voice Recognition

- **Speaker Identification:** Machine vision aids in capturing and analyzing lip movements along with voice features, adding an extra layer of security in voice recognition systems. This multi-modal approach is commonly used in secure phone banking, access control, and call center authentication.
- **Lip Reading for Enhanced Security:** Machine vision analyzes lip movements to verify spoken words, enhancing voice recognition accuracy. This is useful in noisy environments where audio data may be insufficient for reliable identification.

## 7. Hand Geometry Recognition

- Machine vision analyzes hand shapes, including the width, length, and thickness of fingers and the overall hand geometry. Hand geometry recognition is frequently used for time attendance and access control in workplaces, as it is quick, user-friendly, and resistant to duplication.
- Though not as unique as other biometrics like fingerprints or iris patterns, hand geometry provides a fast and effective means of authentication for moderate-security applications.

## 8. Signature Recognition

- **Static Signature Recognition:** Machine vision captures the shape and size of a signature for verification, often used in document validation, financial transactions, and legal processes.
- **Dynamic Signature Recognition:** Machine vision also captures dynamic aspects of signing, such as speed, pressure, and stroke order. This provides a higher level of security and accuracy, as it's challenging to replicate the exact motion of a genuine signature, making it valuable in banking and legal applications.

## 9. DNA Recognition

- Machine vision systems assist in analyzing DNA samples for identity verification, particularly in law enforcement and forensic applications. Though typically used in specialized labs, DNA-based biometrics offer unparalleled accuracy in identifying individuals.
- DNA recognition is valuable in criminal investigations, paternity testing, and immigration cases where high-accuracy identity verification is required.

## 10. Ear Shape Recognition

- Machine vision captures the unique shape and features of an individual's outer ear. Ear recognition is non-intrusive and can be done from a distance, making it suitable for use in surveillance and low-contact authentication applications.
- Since ear shapes are relatively stable over time, ear recognition can serve as a supplementary biometric, especially in multi-modal systems where multiple biometric factors are used for verification.

## 11. Keystroke Dynamics

- Keystroke dynamics involve analyzing typing patterns, such as typing speed, rhythm, and pressure, which vary between individuals. Machine vision can track hand and finger movements while typing, providing an additional behavioral factor for identity verification.
- This method is used for computer access security, online transaction verification, and fraud detection, as it is non-intrusive and doesn't require additional hardware.

## 12. Behavioral Biometrics

- Behavioral biometrics analyze how users interact with devices, including screen swiping, pressure, and rhythm. Machine vision captures these movements in real-time, creating a unique behavioral profile that aids in continuous authentication.
- Behavioral biometrics are used in cybersecurity to detect and prevent identity theft or account takeover by monitoring for atypical behavior in users' interactions.

## 13. Multi-Modal Biometrics

- Multi-modal biometrics use a combination of two or more biometric methods, such as face and fingerprint recognition or voice and lip movement analysis, to improve accuracy and security. Machine vision combines these biometrics seamlessly, providing a robust and flexible solution.
- Multi-modal systems are commonly used in high-security applications, such as border control, secure facility access, and high-value transaction authentication, where multiple layers of verification are necessary.

### Benefits of Machine Vision in Biometrics:

- **Enhanced Accuracy and Security:** Machine vision provides highly accurate biometric identification by capturing and analyzing intricate features that are difficult to replicate, reducing the risk of identity fraud and unauthorized access.
- **Non-Contact and Hygienic:** Many machine vision-based biometrics, such as facial, iris, and gait recognition, are contactless, providing hygienic and convenient options, especially in healthcare and public environments.
- **Real-Time Authentication:** Machine vision systems enable real-time biometric authentication, ensuring rapid verification, crucial in high-traffic environments like airports, banks, and secure facilities.
- **Scalability and Flexibility:** Machine vision-based biometric systems can be scaled to accommodate large databases, making them suitable for nationwide or enterprise-level deployments.
- **Continuous and Passive Verification:** Biometrics like gait and behavior analysis provide continuous and unobtrusive verification, making them ideal for environments where traditional one-time authentication isn't sufficient, such as high-security buildings or online platforms.

Machine vision in biometrics has created more reliable and secure authentication methods across diverse fields, from banking and healthcare to law enforcement and cybersecurity. By capturing and analyzing unique physiological and behavioral traits, machine vision helps ensure that biometric systems are accurate, efficient, and increasingly integral to modern security solutions.

# 2 Mark Questions

### Machine Vision Applications in Manufacturing

1. What are two common machine vision applications in manufacturing?
2. How does machine vision contribute to quality control in manufacturing?

### Machine Vision Applications in Electronics

1. Explain the role of machine vision in PCB inspection.
2. Name two machine vision applications in electronics that enhance assembly line efficiency.

### Machine Vision Applications in Printing

1. Describe how machine vision is used for color accuracy in printing.
2. What is the role of machine vision in label verification in the printing industry?

### Machine Vision Applications in Pharmaceuticals

1. How is machine vision used in pharmaceutical packaging inspection?
2. Name two ways machine vision ensures compliance in pharmaceutical production.

### Machine Vision Applications in Textiles

1. What role does machine vision play in fabric defect detection?
2. Explain how machine vision enhances quality control in textile manufacturing.

### Machine Vision Applications in Non-Visible Spectrum

1. What is one use of infrared machine vision in industrial applications?
2. How does ultraviolet machine vision contribute to surface inspection?

### Machine Vision Applications in Metrology and Gauging

1. Describe a common application of machine vision in metrology.
2. How is machine vision used in dimensional measurement?

### Machine Vision Applications in OCR and OCV

1. Differentiate between OCR and OCV in machine vision.
2. How does machine vision-based OCR improve quality control in packaging?

### Machine Vision in Vision-Guided Robotics

1. What is the importance of machine vision in pick-and-place robotic systems?
2. How does machine vision assist in bin picking in robotics?

## Machine Vision in Field and Service Applications

1. Explain one application of machine vision in power line inspection.
2. How is machine vision used in disaster response?

## Machine Vision in Agriculture

1. Describe the use of machine vision for crop health monitoring.
2. How does machine vision contribute to weed detection in agriculture?

## Machine Vision in Biomedical Field

1. How is machine vision applied in automated blood analysis?
2. Explain the use of machine vision in surgical assistance.

## Machine Vision in Augmented Reality

1. How does machine vision enhance object tracking in augmented reality?
2. Describe the role of machine vision in AR for indoor navigation.

## Machine Vision in Surveillance

1. What is a key benefit of machine vision in crowd counting for surveillance?
2. Describe how machine vision enhances intrusion detection in surveillance.

## Machine Vision in Biometrics

1. Name two biometric applications that rely on machine vision.
2. How does machine vision improve the accuracy of facial recognition systems?

# 15 Mark Questions

1. Explain in detail the various applications of machine vision in manufacturing.
2. Discuss how machine vision enhances quality control, defect detection, and assembly verification, providing specific examples and benefits in manufacturing.
3. Describe the role of machine vision in electronics manufacturing.
4. Explain the applications of machine vision in PCB inspection, component alignment, and defect detection. Discuss the importance of accuracy in electronics and how machine vision contributes to quality.
5. Illustrate the applications of machine vision in the printing industry.
6. Discuss how machine vision systems are used for color matching, label verification, and print quality inspection. Include examples of machine vision improving printing efficiency and consistency.
7. Analyze the significance of machine vision in the pharmaceutical industry.
8. Describe applications in quality control, packaging verification, and compliance. Explain how machine vision ensures product safety and adherence to regulatory standards in pharmaceuticals.
9. Discuss the applications of machine vision in the textile industry and its impact on quality control.
10. Explain how machine vision detects defects, ensures pattern consistency, and inspects fabric textures. Include the advantages of using machine vision for large-scale textile manufacturing.
11. Describe machine vision applications in the non-visible spectrum.
12. Explain how machine vision operates in infrared, ultraviolet, and X-ray spectrums, and provide examples of industries that benefit from each. Discuss the advantages and limitations of using non-visible spectrums in inspection.
13. Explain the role of machine vision in metrology and gauging applications.
14. Discuss how machine vision enhances precision in dimensional measurement, edge detection, and surface inspection. Include examples from industries that rely on high-accuracy metrology.
15. Analyze the applications of OCR and OCV in machine vision.
16. Explain the difference between OCR and OCV and describe how they are used in fields such as packaging, automotive, and document processing. Discuss their importance in ensuring traceability and compliance.
17. Describe machine vision applications in vision-guided robotics.
18. Explain how machine vision enables pick-and-place, sorting, and assembly operations in robotics. Discuss the impact of vision-guided robotics on automation, accuracy, and productivity.
19. Discuss the field and service applications of machine vision in remote or hazardous environments.
20. Explain how machine vision supports infrastructure inspection, utility maintenance, and environmental monitoring. Include examples of its use in power line inspection, disaster response, and hazardous area monitoring.
21. Examine the applications of machine vision in agriculture and its impact on precision farming.
22. Describe the role of machine vision in crop health monitoring, weed detection, and yield estimation. Discuss how these applications contribute to sustainability and resource optimization in agriculture.
23. Discuss the various applications of machine vision in the biomedical field.
24. Explain how machine vision aids in diagnostics, surgery, and laboratory automation. Include applications such as automated cell counting, pathology analysis, and surgical assistance, and discuss its impact on healthcare.
25. Describe how machine vision enhances augmented reality applications.
26. Explain the role of machine vision in object recognition, environment mapping, and gesture tracking in augmented reality. Provide examples from fields like gaming, industrial training, and healthcare.

27.  Analyze the importance of machine vision in surveillance applications.

28.  Describe applications such as facial recognition, intrusion detection, and crowd monitoring in security and public safety. Discuss how machine vision improves response times and situational awareness.

29.  Explain machine vision applications in biometrics and their impact on identity verification.

30.  Discuss biometric methods such as facial recognition, iris scanning, and gait analysis. Explain the benefits and challenges of using machine vision for secure, accurate, and non-intrusive identification.